THE FOOD LOVERS GUIDE
TO THE NORTH WEST

Published by The Bluecoat Press, Liverpool
Edited by Trevor Bates and Claire Walker
Book design by MARCH, Liverpool
Printed by Miro Press

ISBN 1 904438 22 9

Acknowledgments
This book is a first for the region and could not have been compiled without the co-operation and in-depth knowledge of North West Fine Foods (NWFF), the Northwest Fantastic Foods Partnership (FFP), writers, photographers and the proud army of food heroes who strive to win a wider appreciation and recognition for regional produce. The producers are particularly indebted to Peter Papprill, for his guidance and thoughtful comments in the preparation of this book. The support of the Northwest Regional Development Agency (NWDA), the Department for Environment, Food and Rural Affairs (DEFRA), Myerscough College and all contributors is appreciated.

Photography
Thank you to all featured producers who have supplied images to The Bluecoat Press. Images also supplied by David Baxter, NWDA, FFP, NWFF and Made in Cheshire. Additional photography by Amy Cook.

All details in this book are considered to be correct at the time of publication and in accordance with the Northwest Fantastic Foods Partnership. The Bluecoat Press cannot be held responsible for any incorrect information.

THE FOOD LOVERS GUIDE TO THE NORTH WEST

The Bluecoat Press

Northwest
FANTASTIC FOODS
Partnership

CONTENTS

LANCASHIRE by Clarissa Hyman

GREATER MANCHESTER
by Jonathan Schofield

CONTRIBUTORS

Trevor Bates MBE is a former *Daily Telegraph* journalist and launch editor of a number of magazine publications. He also edited *englandsnorthwest*, the first ever words and pictures portrait of the region produced to coincide with the Manchester Commonwealth Games in 2002.

Sandra Allwood is an authority on local cheeses and founder of Ravens Oak Dairy in Cheshire, where she used her farm's organic milk to produce Brie-style cheeses. She has been involved with local foods for the last 20 years and currently works with North West Fine Foods.

Anne Benson has been writing about North West food for a variety of publications including the *Daily Express* and *Daily Post*. She also undertakes restaurant reviews for a number of food guides, including *Dining Out in Wales*.

Christian Dymond is a Cumbria-based freelance writer and TV producer, working for national broadsheet newspapers and BBC Radio 4. He was one of the moving spirits behind the first ever Cumbria and the Lake District Food and Drink Festival in May 2004.

Bob Gledhill is a restaurant journalist known nationally and in the North West for his passion for promoting regional produce. He has collaborated extensively with North West chefs to bring the region's fine food and culinary traditions to a wider audience.

Lynne Greenwood is an accomplished national newspaper and magazine journalist specialising in weekend supplement features including food, lifestyle and property. She is a contributor to *The Daily Telegraph* and *The Times*.

Clarissa Hyman is a food and travel writer based in Manchester. She has written three books. A member of the Guild of Food Writers, she has won several prestigious awards for her writing. She is also active in the Slow Food movement.

Jonathan Schofield writes authoritatively on food and drink for Manchester's *City Life* magazine where he has been guidebooks editor since 2000. He is also a Blue Badge Guide for North West England.

Arthur Taylor writes about regional food, drink, music and customs in Britain and Europe. He has several awards from the British Guild of Beer Writers and was Glenfiddich Drinks Writer of the Year in 2001.

Carol Wilson is a Cheshire-based food/cookery writer with a number of books to her credit, including *Porters English Cookery Bible, Ancient and Modern*. She is particularly interested in regional recipes and culinary traditions throughout the world and is an enthusiastic supporter of small traditional food producers.

This book offers a culinary tour through North West England's five counties: Cumbria, Lancashire, Greater Manchester, Merseyside and Cheshire.

Map: NWDA

NORTH WEST FANTASTIC FOODS

THIS BOOK IS ABOUT MUCH MORE than just food and drink. It is the result of a combination of influences: local farmers, local pride, historical boundaries and even the Foot and Mouth outbreak.

In the recent past food projects have been started by enthusiastic groups to sing the praises of local food, only to find themselves often competing against each other and duplicating effort. Their efforts would place neighbour against neighbour, and county against county. Yes, there were some stunning successes but, more often than not, the important messages were lost, as attention fell on the more organised regions who shouted louder. The rich heritage of farming and local specialised foods in the North West of England was a very local secret.

Foot and Mouth changed all that. Suddenly the only way to survive was to pull together. With true northern grit and determination from all sides, even as many lost their livelihoods, survival was exactly what happened.

The creation of a single-minded, united partnership between all the food initiatives across the North West of England was deemed an impossible goal by many. Local pride would stop it, bureaucracy would hinder it. But here we are, all working together and at last producing a book that starts to tell the story of the fantastic foods and producers to be found across the region. It's a journey many have joined – the producers themselves, local government, the Northwest Regional Development Agency, the Department for Environment, Food and Rural Affairs, the existing local and regional food projects, and Myerscough College, who now administer the whole effort.

Under the banner of the Fantastic Foods Partnership all the local and regional initiatives work to one end: to assist local and speciality food and drink producers to develop their business and market their products. It's a simple remit but it has taken a mammoth effort to make it work and like all good cheeses, the longer it is allowed to mature, the better it becomes. Our thanks go to all who have put the effort into compiling this book. We hope it will help you enjoy the tastes and delights of the fantastic foods on offer across the North West. After all, the secret's out now!

Lorna M Tyson

Lorna Tyson MBE
Chair of the Fantastic Foods Partnership

FOREWORD

THERE IS NOTHING BETTER IN THE WORLD of gingerbread than Grasmere Gingerbread. And there it is being produced in a particular part of Cumbria, one of a whole range of speciality foods in the North West that I believe are just waiting to leap on to the national stage.

For too long the Lancashire hotpot has had to shoulder the burden of the North West's culinary reputation nationally. But now, because of the desire of farmers, producers, chefs, shoppers – anyone who likes food – to grow and seek out high quality, regional specialities, the picture is changing.

This book celebrates that renaissance. It highlights the quality and distinctiveness of North West foods from the farm to the fork, from prize-winning territorial cheeses and artisan bakers, to talented chefs and hugely varied farmers' markets. And it offers local people and tourists valuable signposting on where to buy and where to eat some of the best foods in Britain.

My love of food started because I grew up in a family that liked to eat. We also travelled a lot and the more you travel, the more interested you become in food, whether you are travelling within a region, or across a country. People now have a greater desire to travel to places which have interesting food, to search out that food, to find out where it comes from, to eat that food, to buy it and take it home as a souvenir.

Of course, there have always been regional differences within the UK. Even at a time when the nation was less sophisticated in terms of the foods it was demanding, it was easy to draw a map of the country divided into the regions where people used brown sauce and those where people did not. Another classic example of regional differences is that between northern and southern fish and chips – the type of fish, the way it is prepared and the way it is cooked.

The growing awareness of regional identity has heightened the move to rediscover and highlight regional foodstuffs. Just as the variety in food and drink that makes travelling from region to region in Italy or France a pure culinary pleasure, so in the UK there is a growing desire to celebrate the differences between the regions.

It is partly a reaction to the homogenisation of the 1990s – wherever we travelled we found the same shops, the same brands, the same identities, the same tastes. And while that inevitably raised standards, it prompted a longing to find foods that were distinctive and different.

Foot and Mouth disease was also influential. When there is public concern about the food chain, people rightly become more interested in the pedigree and traceability of foods they are eating, whether it be a scone or a lamb chop. The epidemic also exposed an underlying weakness in the rural economy, whose revival and redevelopment includes a new concentration on specialist, high quality, added value foods and products.

And people nowadays like to talk about food – 30 years ago they just ate it with little comment. While there isn't much to say about a lump of cheese produced in a factory, you can talk about a particular type of Cheshire cheese made in a traditional way by a farmer using his own dairy milk.

Restaurants are reinforcing the desire for distinctive regional tastes too. At last when you go into restaurants in Britain you are more likely to be offered a fantastic selection of English cheeses for example. Increasingly, restaurants, chefs and discerning diners are interested in the provenance of the foods on the menu.

People are prepared to pay a premium for foods which are high quality and distinctive. As a friend said as he explained why new millionaires buy Ferraris, 'It still remains a relatively cheap luxury!' In the case of food, if you pay a little extra for half a kilo of cheese which is twice as good as the cheaper option, it is a relatively small investment for a relatively big gain.

And within the North West, there are more than a few Epicurean gains to be made. For one of the great features of the region is its huge diversity. Stretching from Chester to Hadrian's Wall, it includes the most incredible concentration of high-quality urban architecture in Liverpool and Manchester, as well as the most magnificent natural beauty of the Lake District. There is everything in the North West. So what better place to embark on a food trail, a food pilgrimage, starting with that Grasmere Gingerbread.

Loyd Grossman

Culinary Jewels
of the North West

THE FERTILE COUNTRYSIDE, COASTLINE AND INDUSTRIAL TOWNS of the North West of England have a strong culinary heritage and offer an extraordinary variety of delicious foods. The skill and wisdom of the region's artisan food and drink producers, together with the freshest top quality produce have ensured that the North West forms an important part of England's culinary map. Some specialities such as Cheshire cheese have gone on to become internationally famous, whilst others, such as Goosnargh cakes, generally remain known only within the region.

The wealth of delicious and unique food specialities gradually developed over generations and largely depended on the ingredients available in the region. For instance, potato was Lancashire's main crop and was used in a wide variety of savoury and sweet dishes such as potato cakes and farmhouse pudding (a sweet boiled pudding made with mashed potatoes, carrots, dried fruits and spices). Oats, easily cultivated in the northern climate, were grown locally and treacle and unrefined sugar from the West Indies were easily obtainable from ports on the Cumberland coast and Liverpool.

North West farmers have always taken great pride in their livestock and their efforts produce flavoursome, tender meat. The ancient Herdwick (meaning 'sheep pasture') breed thrive on the Cumbrian moorland, enjoying a diet rich in heather and bilberries, which impart a rich, slightly gamey flavour to the mutton and lamb. Beatrix Potter bred these hardy sheep in her later career as a Cumbrian hill farmer. The animal's long straight bones were ideal for standing upright around the sides of the deep pots used to make the region's appetising stews, such as Cumberland tatie pot and Lancashire hotpot.

Another kind of tasty meat stew is scouse, which gave its name to the inhabitants of Liverpool. Originally a shipboard dish, it may have been brought to Liverpool by Scandanavian sailors, who called the dish 'labskaus' and 'lapskojs', respectively. It can be made with beef or lamb, with the addition of potatoes, carrots and onions. Pickled beetroot is the traditional accompaniment in Merseyside. 'Blind' scouse is made with just vegetables, minus the meat.

Lancaster, one of the North West's towns and cities that have preserved a long tradition of home cooking and baking.

Beef, lamb and pork have been enjoyed in the region for generations and every part of the animal was used in a rich variety of dishes. All types of offal (rarely seen in other parts of the country) were, and indeed still are, popular today; tripe (the stomach lining of a cow) is often served with onions. Other offal includes chitterlings (pigs' intestines turned inside-out, cleaned, plaited and boiled), elder (cows' pressed udder), lambs' fry (testicles), sweetbreads, pigs' trotters and cow-heel. These last two are used to enrich stews and pies and produce an excellent jellied stock. Black puddings, their deep garnet interiors studded with white fat, and enclosed in shiny black casings, have a rich, spicy flavour and are a great favourite. Recipes vary according to the maker and are jealously guarded; Bury black puddings are particularly renowned. You can buy a hot black pudding to savour as you wander round Bury market – there's even a reduced fat version for weight watchers!

North West butchers are also deservedly proud of their magnificent range of sausages, such as the celebrated meaty Cumberland sausage (which has the distinctive feature of being made in one piece rather than being twisted into links) and superb, succulent, richly-flavoured hams, including a recently introduced Parma-style, air-dried ham.

The region's lush pastures provide rich grazing for dairy cattle, delivering milk that is ideal for the internationally renowned Cheshire and Lancashire cheeses. A wide variety of vegetables and fruits were also cultivated in rural areas and any surplus was thriftily used to make a tempting variety of jams, chutneys and pickles. A particular Westmorland speciality is the damson (a variety of plum). Known locally as 'Witherslacks', damsons are used to make a fruity beer. The blackish purple fruits ripen in September and are sold from roadside stalls and in local shops and markets.

The introduction of the railways in the nineteenth century and the new vogue for sea bathing, saw visitors flocking to the seaside towns of Southport and Morecambe, where fish was so plentiful that the *Liverpool Courier* reported that 'Lovers of good eating may abundantly gratify their appetites with turbot, salmon, sole oysters, shrimps and sometimes with the John Dory'.

These towns still maintain their long tradition of potting sea-fresh shrimps and methods have changed little, although tractors are now used to haul the nets ashore instead of horses and carts. The tiny shellfish are boiled in seawater, quickly cooled and peeled, then enhanced with butter and a touch of mace and nutmeg, before being packed into tubs or pots.

The North West's industrial towns and cities have preserved a long tradition of home cooking and baking. Many recipes came into being during the Industrial Revolution when the families of mill workers and miners

Farmhouse Fare

Sticky toffee pudding, moist and smothered in a lusciously rich toffee sauce, a treat now in demand all over the world.

depended on nourishing dishes such as stews, pies and puddings. Women set aside a baking day every week and produced enough cakes, pies and bread to last the week.

These humble treats have become specialities of the region and many have delightful names such as Cumberland Rum Nicky (a pie with a rich sticky filling of dates, ginger, brown sugar and rum), sly cakes (similar to Cumberland Rum Nickies) and love paste (a type of shortbread filled with jam). Others were named after their place of origin. Goosnargh cakes, with their thick sugary crust, are a speciality of Preston and were originally flavoured with coriander and caraway seeds. Eccles cakes, a mouth-watering combination of currants, sugar and spices in crisp, buttery flaky pastry were once associated with the fairs or 'wakes' in the area. Chorley cakes are similar, but are made with shortcrust pastry.

Treacle (a by-product of sugar refining), sugar and ginger arrived on ships in the busy ports such as Liverpool and Whitehaven and were quickly incorporated into recipes for pies, puddings and cakes. Grasmere Gingerbread, from the town of the same name, is a 'short' crumbly gingerbread with a powerful ginger flavour, originally made with locally grown oats or oatmeal. Crisp Ormskirk gingerbread can still be sampled in the town's street markets.

Rum butter, a delectable combination of butter, dark rum, sugar and nutmeg, has been associated with Cumberland since the eighteenth century, when it was given to pregnant women during their confinement and after giving birth to speed their recovery. Nowadays it is the traditional accompaniment to Christmas pudding and mince pies.

The cuisine of the region constantly continues to evolve and develop, with imaginative food producers incorporating new ingredients, ideas and cooking methods. Sticky toffee pudding from Cartmel in the Lake District is a fairly recent innovation and soon had many imitators, but none are as good as the original, which is made with free range eggs and cream. The moist puddings, smothered in a lusciously rich toffee sauce, are now in demand all over the world.

Thanks to the recent renewal of interest and demand for 'real' food, full of flavour, these culinary jewels of the North West have survived to become a valuable part of the region's history.

A Rich Tradition
of Cheesemaking

FFP

TODAY, AT THE BEGINNING OF THE TWENTY-FIRST CENTURY, mention the word cheese with no other descriptor and most of us would think of Cheddar, which far outsells all the other British territorials. But it was not always so. Until the First World War 'cheese' meant Cheshire, which at that time was still responsible for well over 50 per cent of the English market.

The North West has always been a region rich in cheese-making; the climate suits grass growing and the dairy cow, which facilitates milk production. Cheshire is the oldest named cheese in the British Isles, predating the Romans and mentioned in the *Domesday Book*. Originally this type of cheese was made all over Cheshire and Lancashire, as well as Shropshire and parts of the Midlands and North Wales. Gradually, between the tenth and eighteenth centuries, Lancashire developed as a cheese in its own right, although production was primarily small scale. Thus two of the great cheeses of Britain are part of our heritage today.

Cheshire's heyday was in the eighteenth century. Farmers needed a means of preserving their milk and before refrigeration was available, turning it into cheese was the obvious solution. It is the salt underlying this area that gives the cheese its salty tang and it is imperative to the flavour. One of the first by-products of cheese was whey butter, which can still sometimes be found in Cheshire. The cheeses were ripened on straw in darkened rooms, and when ready were sold at weekly cheese fairs – almost every town of any size had one (in Nantwich they continued until the 1930s). The cheeses were then transported down the canals to the Midlands, or to Liverpool, from where they were sent by ship to London. If a farmer was very lucky he might find a 'green fade' amongst his store; these naturally, but unpredictably occurring, blue cheeses, were sought after and highly prized.

Gradually, sales of farmhouse Cheshire declined; railways made it easier to transport fresh milk to urban areas and the first creamery (a small factory) in the county opened in 1875. In 1914, there were still over 2,000 farms making Cheshire, by 1939 there were just 405; in 1982 there were 18 farms in the MMB Farmhouse Grading Scheme, and today there are probably fewer than 5 farms still producing this fantastic cheese in the traditional way.

Today's Cheshires are available in Red, White and Blue. John Bourne's family has been producing handmade Cheshire at The Bank, Malpas, since 1930. Today he makes all three varieties from pasteurised, unpasteurised or organic milk. His Blue is unique in that he adds no blue culture to his vat, but chooses what he considers to be suitable specimens, and then puts them in his cellar to let nature take its course. Some are more blue than others, depending on conditions, but their flavour is truly superb. John often has more mature cheeses on offer for those who like a bit of bite. The Wades of Mollington are another farming family with a long tradition of making Cheshire and they also have a choice of Red, White and Blue. Chris makes his Blues with modern cultures, keeping diversity alive, for these excellent cheeses are very different from Bourne's.

Tip When shopping for Cheshire cheese, what should we be looking for? The flavour and aroma should be clean, mild, slightly acidic and slightly salty; more mature cheeses become tangy with age. Cheshire should be moderately firm with an open crumbly texture. White Cheshire should be bright white and Red Cheshire should be a bright and even pale orange.

Lancashire, the second great cheese of the North West, came close to disappearing. It has always been very popular in its own county and fairly so in the region, but very little known elsewhere. In 1995, Mrs Kirkham's Lancashire was entered in the British Cheese Awards – without her knowledge – and won Supreme Champion! As a result, this cheese has been steadily growing in popularity. Traditionally, the cheese has always been made on a reasonably small scale because of its method, which involves taking curd from three days' cheese-making and combining it. Like Cheshire, it is produced from whole milk, and butter was made from its whey. Today, only two makers still use the three-day method, although several more use two-day curd. Combining curds of different ages creates a crumbly textured, slightly stippled, creamy-coloured cheese with an extra dimension in taste.

Tip Lancashire can be found as 'Creamy', which is moist, mild and young, or 'Tasty' which is strong, sharp and aged. 'Crumbly' Lancashire was created after the Second World War. It is quickly made from one day's curd and has an acidic bite. It should be eaten young.

Britain in general has seen an explosion of interest in cheeses; old recipes have been revived and there are a growing number of exciting artisan cheesemakers. One innovation in Lancashire has been the development of blue cheeses. Dew-lay have produced Garstang Blue, wonderful, creamy and reminiscent of a Dolcelatte. Butlers have created Blacksticks Blue, deep golden-coloured and slightly firmer, originally based on an old recipe, but which has evolved its own distinctive identity.

Britain has seen an explosion of interest in cheeses; old recipes have been revived and there are a growing number of exciting artisanal cheesemakers.

FFP

Some cheesemakers have looked at continental favourites and experimented. Ravens Oak Dairy, near Nantwich, produce Burland Green, an organic brie, made from their own milk. It is butter-coloured with a hint of Cheshire salt in the taste and a soft, squidgy texture. Using locally purchased milks, the dairy also produces goat, water buffalo and sheep milk bries as well as a range of fresh cheeses.

Carolyn Fairburn from Thornby Moor in Cumbria also uses milk from cows, goats and sheep to produce a range of cheeses, both hard and soft. She is an innovative cheesemaker in an area not traditionally associated with cheese. In the Lake District a type of cheese was made in many cottages, indeed Wordsworth refers to cottagers' cheese, but unlike their southern neighbours, butter was made first and the resulting buttermilk then used for the cheese, producing a rather tough result.

We are fortunate to have several champions of our cheeses in the region. Two in particular are inspiring: Peter Papprill, the Cheese Detective, is very supportive of producers and sends their wares off to many of the country's finest chefs, as well as introducing our cheeses to a wider audience through his speaking engagements, while Carole Faulkner from the Cheese Shop, Chester, never stops encouraging her many customers from all over Britain and beyond to sample local delights. Farmers' markets, farm shops and food festivals are wonderful places to search out exciting local cheeses and enjoy a tradition that goes back to the Romans and before.

New Variations on a Growing Theme

Flavour Fresh Tomatoes and NWFF

IF KENT IS THE GARDEN OF ENGLAND, then the North West is its market garden and salad bowl. For many years, before modern irrigation techniques changed the way people farmed, the areas around Lancashire and parts of Merseyside, as well as Cheshire, provided the perfect conditions for growing vegetables and salads for the whole country.

The reasons for this are much the same as why wines fare better in some places than others; it is the vegetable version of terroir – the combination of soil, climate and, formerly, easy access to markets.

The Black Moss soils around Ormskirk, Halsall, Tarleton, Chatmoss and Earlham are considered the best peat soils in the country. Lancashire potatoes were revered as the soil produced a good clean skin finish; while in Cheshire, the country's most northerly crop of early potatoes is produced as the soil warms up quickly; thanks to the microclimate around Frodsham and south of Warrington.

Fruit is not neglected in the region; the picturesque Lyth Valley in Cumbria is renowned for its damsons. They are a little smaller and sharper than others further south and throughout September they are sold locally at roadside stalls and in shops. The damsons are turned into jams, ice creams, gin, beer, cakes and even cheese. In April, a special damson day is held when thousands of visitors arrive to taste the fruits of last season's crop.

Gradually, vegetable and salad farmers began to face increasing competition and an over saturation of the market. Some went out of business but others have fought back by diversifying. Harvest, a group of growers made up of small family businesses, is working in conjunction with Sharrock's Fresh Produce, based in Preston, to find new and interesting products to sell.

It was to Sharrock's that leading chef Nigel Haworth, from Northcote Manor in Lancashire, turned to when he was looking for someone to grow Golden Beetroot. On a trip to California he had tried this sweet-tasting beet and wanted to find someone who could supply him back home. Farmer Peter Ascroft, whose family have farmed in Tarleton since the turn of the last century, agreed to take on the challenge. Booths, which has supermarket stores across Lancashire and Cheshire, was then brought in to sell it. Also through Sharrock's, David Fryer, in Warrington, is now growing Yukon Gold potatoes, after an American chef visiting the region started extolling their virtues as the ideal potato for making chips.

Booths

One of the delights about vegetables grown in the North West is the freshness.

Booths is well known for its championing of local produce and they stock Cavolo Nero, the dark green Tuscan speciality, which is now being grown by the Molyneux family of Ormskirk. Though they keep their core business of growing fresh greens, sprouts and green cabbage, the family diversified into trying out this Italian version four years ago.

Peter Eminson, of Tarleton, was looking to do something different when he was introduced to Pak Choi, which he can grow under glass in winter time, thus extending his growing season throughout the year. There is even a northerly watercress grower, James Duerdon, near Great Eccleston, in Lancashire.

Some specialise in seasonal produce. Joy Waugh, in Carlisle, uses most of the vegetables grown on her farm to make soup, which she sells at farmers' markets. But she sells yellow courgettes and runner beans, in season, as she finds people cannot get hold of them easily and they are particularly popular.

For John Williamson, of Crewe, it was people knocking on his door after seeing the maize in his field and asking if they could buy some, which made him realise there was a niche in the market for sweetcorn. He now grows six varieties, so they all ripen at different times, and Early Bird, which is a very sweet strain, won an award at the North West Producer of the Year Awards 2003. During the autumn he sells from his farm shop and has regulars coming back year after year.

The Wareings have been in the farming business since 1910 at Tarleton and grow about 40 different varieties of vegetables, but they have now gone in for farmers' markets in a big way – visiting 15 across the region every month. They use the markets to sell more unusual varieties such as celeriac, purple sprouting broccoli, pink fir apple potatoes, Swiss ruby chard and red cauliflowers in summer, as they find it gives them the chance to talk to customers and explain how to cook and use them.

One of the delights about this fantastic produce being grown in the North West is the freshness. By buying direct from the producer, or through box schemes, local shops, or through www.northernharvest.co.uk a specialist website selling local produce, you know that it has not been long out of the soil, that it has not been flown thousands of miles, nor picked before it is ready or ripened artificially.

In fact, pick-your-owns, which proliferate throughout the region during the summer months, are a fun way to ensure that just plucked flavour and to teach children about where their food comes from and how good it can be, and thanks to the vegetable terroir, local North West vegetables taste just that little bit superior.

The Rise of the Artisan Baker

Amy Cook

THERE IS NOTHING LIKE THE ENTICING SMELL and taste of a fresh, home-baked loaf. Bread is the ultimate comfort food and its variations are myriad. Think of cutting through the crusty outer shell of a farmhouse loaf; the slightly tart, but gloriously chewy texture of sourdough; the fulfilling mouthful of a crunchy granary, or a soft, floury ciabatta melting on the tongue.

Sadly the real taste of bread has largely been lost in the price-driven switch to mass market production. The real beauty of a fresh loaf is the care, tenderness and time it takes to make. Good bread should have an uneven texture, a gloriously wholesome taste and should not be inedible after just one day.

But the good news is that there is a renaissance happening in the world of bread and in the North West the number of artisan bakers is beginning to grow – bringing back the true meaning of baking. Behind them are the increasing numbers of discerning customers demanding more from their daily loaf.

An artisan baker is a craftsperson highly trained in mixing, fermenting, shaping and baking a handcrafted loaf of bread. It takes a dedicated type of person to become a baker, rising very early, or working through the night to ensure that a sufficient supply of quality fresh bread is available for shoppers first thing in the morning. These are the true food heroes.

The first and most legendary artisan baker in the North West is Andrew Whitley, a former BBC Russian Service producer, who went to Cumbria in search of the simpler life and set up the Village Bakery in 1976, now something of a national institution. Originally the wood-fired brick oven – the breadmaker's ultimate toy that helped to make the bakery famous – was built because the stone barn they had converted in Melmerby did not have a power supply.

The aim was to produce wholemeal bread from organic English wheat, an interesting challenge in the synthetic world of the 1970s, when white sliced bread was king. But it worked and now the Village Bakery is famous across the UK for its organic bread, supplying a wide range of retail outlets and offering an on-line mail order service.

Since Andrew's success, more craft/artisan bakers have opened throughout the region, producing bread from carefully sourced English ingredients and using time-honoured methods.

Lee Hollywood, who set up Born and Bread, in Liscard, Wirral, could have followed in his brother's footsteps and become a TV cook but he wanted to return to his roots, to bake and to be hands on. Now he is looking to expand, keen to acquire a bigger bakery where he can start running bread-making courses.

Simon Thomas has bread-making in his blood, taught by his mother and grandmother, he always made his own; so the shop-bought bread he discovered at university came as something of a shock. He started making his own again and even traded loaves with fellow students for some of their homebrew. Eventually this led to him opening a café where he again made all the bread fresh every day. As more and more people came just to buy his loaves, he and his wife decided to go with the flow, gave up the café and started selling bread at WI Markets, before finding the right premises for a baker's shop, the Staff of Life, in Kendal, five years ago. He believes bread-making knows no bounds and it can be as wild as the baker's imagination.

Amy Cook

Artisan bread is made with love and care, using skills and knowledge passed down for generations.

Someone who would agree with him is Aidan Monks. Chat to Aidan for a few minutes and you will soon be swept away by his enthusiasm. This is a man who knows his bread, which shows by the success of his Le Pain de Paris business in Staveley Mill, Kendal. Here he uses a stone based oven, which delivers instant heat direct to the dough, creating a bread with a unique flavour, texture and most importantly, a good crust. Aidan will tell you that soft bread is not necessarily good bread, as the flavour comes through the crust.

The many different cultures who have made their home in the North West have brought their traditional bread-making skills with them. Mr Zaremba, from Krakow, opened Barbakan, in Chorlton, South Manchester, in 1964, using methods learned in his homeland. This independent shop produces more than 40 different types of hand-moulded bread from cheese and bacon loaves to San Francisco sourdough.

Restaurants are also realising that it is a crime to spoil quality food with inferior bread. Marc Verité, of the Warehouse Brasserie in Southport has his own in-house bakery courtesy of his father Claude, who has many years of bread-making experience. Customers were so impressed that they now often pop in just to buy the bread and a shop counter has been set up at the front of the restaurant.

Artisan bread is made with love and care, using skills and knowledge passed down for generations. Good bread, like quality wine, takes time to develop and these bakers are willing to take that time. Whether you eat it on its own, use it to create a chunky bacon sandwich, or serve it just with cheese, it is something to celebrate and savour down to the very last crumb.

Sweet Heart of the Region

Amy Cook

WHEN GEORGE FORMBY SANG about his little stick of Blackpool rock, he was playing on two good old northern themes: saucy humour and sticky sweets. This fondness for a good gobstopper still distinguishes our palate, even if most sweet shops have merged into newsagents or morphed into the pick 'n' mix stands of mall and market. But dig a little deeper and you'll find marvellous, old fashioned regional specialities such as those made by Stockley's Sweets of Oswaldtwistle, many still dispensed from glass jars, lined up in a mass of bright colour and tempting, tiny shapes: Herbal Candy, Pear Drops, Winter Nips, Cinder Toffee and the world-famous Coltsfoot Rock.

The North West can also claim a few Golds in any national confectionery Hall of Fame. The husband and wife team of Barker and Dobson, for example, began trading in Liverpool in 1834, and their grandsons, Henry and Percy, were the first in the country to introduce individually wrapped sweets. Chewy, pillow-shaped Everton Mints (or toffees) in their football strip colours were always their most popular product.

From marvellous old fashioned regional specialities to fabulous new varieties, there is an assortment of artisan sweet producers in the North West.

Other notables include Kendal Mint Cake, every hiker's stand-by, famously taken up Everest by Chris Bonnington; fabulous toffee and fudge from the Penrith Toffee Shop, handmade in batches and packed into gilt-edged white boxes inscribed with copperplate lettering; and Uncle Joe's Mint Balls which, as everyone from Wigan to New York's West Side knows, keep you all aglow. A grand roll-call, now joined by newcomers such as Salmesbury-based, Susan's Farmhouse Fudge.

Many sweets have medicinal roots, and once were as much a part of the apothecary's as the confectioner's art. The famous Fishermen's Friends lozenges were a local pharmacist's concoction to help sooth the sore throats of Fleetwood fishermen, brought on by lengthy exposure to North Sea cold and fog. Curiously (and fortunately), Fishermen's Friends are now enjoyed by people from countries around the world as a sweet rather than a cure.

Arguably, some of this expertise in sugar craft developed as a result of the sugar cane imported in the eighteenth century from the West Indies into the

Atlantic trade ports of the Cumbrian coast. It could also be argued that the extreme hardship of life in the Lancashire factories and mill towns needed a little sweetening. These simple pleasures were a cheap and energy-boosting way to buck up the spirits of factory and textile mill workers. They may also have been an occasional substitute for the temptations of the demon drink: the Temperance Movement persisted in the North West long after it declined elsewhere. And sweets, especially sticks of rock, were an inexpensive souvenir of the annual day or wakes week seaside trip. Minty Blackpool rock, famed in Donald McGill postcards, is made in all manner of novelty shapes, but when it comes to irresistible, jaw-breaking, tooth-rotting, pulled sugar pleasure, you still can't beat that shocking pink telescope with the town's name running through the core.

Chocolate arrived late in Britain and the North West, only becoming an important sweetmeat in the mid-nineteenth century. The region was never part of the mass market industry, but in more recent years a whole assortment of artisan producers have set up shop here. A beautiful blue box packed with handmade continental chocolates from Sarjeants of Hoylake is an instant way-to-a-girl's-heart present, while Cheshire chocoholics can stock up on Freudenberg Swiss truffles at The Old Fire Station Chocolate Shop in Tarporley. Moving north, Slattery's of Whitefield offer strawberry chocolate pigs, Belgian truffles and courses on chocolate-making. You can watch fabulous varieties such as Lime and Thyme or Honey and Coconut being made at the Rheged Visitor Centre by Saunders of Penrith; and at Orton in Cumbria, few will be able to resist leaving with at least one handmade rum truffle or three under their belts from Kennedy's Fine Chocolates.

In fact, there must be something in the North West air that stimulates chocolate cravings. The Old Smokehouse in Penrith makes chocolate truffles with fresh fruit and local cream; Chocolat in Kirkby Lonsdale sell a fine range of English, French and Belgian chocolates; last, but certainly not least, 1657 Chocolate House in Kendal is the ne plus ultra of chocolate shops, guaranteed to produce paralysis of indecision in the face of 395 varieties plus 32 types of drinking chocolate.

As our Mr Formby once said, count your blessings and smile.

In Praise of the Humble Sausage

WE EAT A STAGGERING FIVE MILLION SAUSAGES every day in the UK, proof, if it were needed, that they are one of the nation's all time favourite foods.

Amazingly versatile, sausages can be enjoyed for breakfast, lunch, dinner and snacks, as well as at picnics and barbecues. The recent emergence of speciality sausages in a variety of tantalising flavours (pheasant and wild boar; duck and orange; steak and Guinness and venison and wild mushroom, to name but a few!) has resulted in new, gourmet-style dishes, with a touch more sophistication than good old bangers and mash. Incidentally, sausages were called bangers during World War II, because they contained so much water that they exploded when fried!

Venison sausages are just one of 400 varieties available.

The Romans introduced sausages and black puddings to Britain. Highly spiced and seasoned with herbs, some were ready to cook as soon as they were made, whilst others were smoked for a long time beforehand. Sausages were a nutritious portable food for the marching legions and an ideal way of using up the bits and pieces left over from an animal carcass.

The conquering Normans later introduced their varieties into our cuisine and sausages soon became an established staple food throughout Britain whether boiled, grilled or fried. Seventeenth century innovations were the dividing of sausages into links and the introduction of the skinless sausage.

There are now more than 400 sausage varieties, but Cumberland is still considered the meatiest. A chunky, coarse-cut sausage, spiced with black pepper, it is traditionally made in a continuous spiral and is sold by length rather than weight.

Richard Woodall, a family business that has flourished in Cumbria for almost 200 years, choose best quality pork from their own herd of pigs and a special blend of herbs and spices to make their succulent Waberthwaite Cumberland sausages. The sausage is a favourite of the royal family and the company is the proud holder of a Royal Warrant.

Cranstons is another family enterprise justly proud of its Cumbrian roots and its sausages. From modest beginnings in Penrith in 1914, the company has developed a thriving chain of shops based throughout the region and uses only freshest quality produce for its sausages. Varieties include Lamb, Apple and Rosemary, Honey and Mustard, Turkey and Cranberry, Pork and Leek and a gluten-free Farmhouse sausage. In 2003 the company carried off the Best Cumberland Sausage Award in the North West Producer of the Year Competition. Cranstons continually strive to introduce new varieties and welcome suggestions from customers.

Alan Jackson Butchers in Alderley Edge, Cheshire, make around ten varieties, all from Gloucester Old Spot (the only breed of pork sold in the shop). There's also a gluten-free sausage containing potato powder, a filler that works well, as the sausages cook with little fat loss and almost no shrinkage. Other varieties include Pork and Leek and very tasty Wild Boar. Unlike pork, wild boar is a red meat with a slightly gamey flavour.

Steadmans, based in Sedbergh, Cumbria, and one of Rick Stein's 'Food Heroes', make a mouth-watering range of award-winning sausages. Their best seller is the superb Ravenstonedale Red, a Gold award-winner made with Garsdale pork, garlic, cheddar and herbs. Their Dales Farmhouse sausage and Lamb and Rosemary sausages won Silver Awards, while their Oriental Pork with cashew nuts was a Platinum award-winner in the national winners-only invitation competition at the NEC at Birmingham March 2002. They were the runner-up at the 1999 World Cumberland Sausage Championship at Carlisle.

Tip When buying sausages look for plumpness and a high meat content (70 per cent or more) and natural skins. British pork has some of the highest standards in the world. The sausages will be clearly marked as British Pork or will carry the Quality Standard Mark or the Little Red Tractor Mark.

Sausages can be made with any meat, but most sausages eaten in the UK are made with pork meat, fat, a cereal filler, water, herbs and spices. Sausages made with organic and rare breed meats are particularly good and are growing in popularity. At the 2003 Great Taste Awards, sausages made with rare breed pork won the Gold medal.

Quality sausages may contain twice as much lean meat (some are 100 per meat) than a cheaper version – so it's well worth paying extra. Today, grilling is the most popular cooking method (used for 44 per cent of all sausages) followed by frying (23 per cent) and baking (20 per cent). Whichever method you choose, never prick sausages; they should be done slowly (to ensure that the skins do not burst) until cooked right through, but still juicy. Sausages don't cook well on the fierce heat of a barbecue. Almost everyone has experienced sausages which are charred on the outside and unpleasantly raw inside. If you're cooking them for a barbecue, the trick is to poach them in boiling water first for 30 minutes and then barbecue them for 10 minutes or so, to brown them and add that unique barbecue flavour.

John Rudden, chef and co-owner of the White Hart Inn in Lydgate, Oldham, has won many awards for his excellent cooking. After a stint at several fine restaurants, including the prestigious Arkle restaurant in the Chester Grosvenor Hotel, John went to the White Hart as a chef and was asked to become a partner in the business.

Sausages are John's passion and he devises all the recipes himself leaving a butcher in his production kitchen to make the sausages exactly to his specifications. John says that the secret of a good sausage is to use top quality ingredients and his sausages are certainly much in demand locally. He sells around 400 every week, although this can double in busy periods.

Currently the menu at the White Hart features five varieties of meaty sausages: Pork and Leek; Cumberland, Lamb and Mint, Saddleworth (with chicken and black pudding) and the Manchester Sausage, a spicy pork sausage made to a recipe found in an eighty-year-old book on sausages and sausage-making. There are also nine different types of mashed potatoes to choose from to accompany the tasty sausages, including horseradish, spinach and black pudding and cheese. John is working on a couple of new sausage recipes at present – Chicken, Tomato and Feta and a Lamb and Cassoulet, made with lamb, beans and herbs, for which he's trying to source some local Saddleworth lamb.

All John's delicious gourmet-style sausages are available to buy from the White Hart Inn in 450g packs.

Cradle of Fish and Chips

Amy Cook

WHEN CELEBRITY CHEF ANTONY WORRALL THOMPSON spent time in the jungle courtesy of television's *I'm a Celebrity – Get Me Out of Here!* one of the dishes he really craved was a big portion of fish and chips washed down with a cup of tea. Millions of people in the UK agree with his description of fish and chips as 'real food – a hearty and nutritious meal'. In fact, 23,648,000 portions of the stuff were eaten in North West England alone in 2002.

Although the genius who first matched fish with chips remains elusive and even the identity of the first fish and chip shop is a slippery customer, the North West is one of the main contenders for the title of 'cradle of fish and chips'.

Today it can rightfully boast some of the best fish and chips in the country, producing that unmistakable smell which sets the taste buds tingling. Those who are passionate about cooking (and eating) fish and chips all have their

Amy Cook

The North West can boast some of the best fish and chips in the country.

own favourite 'chippy'. The first shops to add fish to chips in the North West appeared in the late 1860s – 25 years after Charles Dickens mentioned a 'fried fish warehouse' in *Oliver Twist* – and the combination quickly spread through the cotton towns of Lancashire.

The fish was first fried in cottonseed oil but later, overwhelmingly in vegetable oils and even later, in Manchester, fish and chips were often accompanied by mushy peas and a glass of Vimto, the fruit cordial made in the city. By the 1950s fish and chip shops were providing a hot lunchtime meal for thousands who worked in the mills and factories across the region. Apprentices would deliver the orders in the morning for lunchtime collection.

Today there are still more than 8,500 fish and chip shops in the UK and the industry enjoys a turnover of £900 million. Cod is the most popular fish, accounting for more than 60 per cent of fish sold, and is first choice in the North West. Les Manning and his wife Michelle, who own three fish and chip shops in the region – all called Les's Fish Bar – have earned national recognition for the quality of their food. In 2000, his shop and restaurant in Crewe was the national winner in the annual Fish and Chip Shop of the Year Competition, organised by the Sea Fish Industry Authority. And in 2003 it was runner-up in the regional contest, pipped to the title by Les's Fish Bar in Widnes, co-owned by his brother-in-law Andrew Nield and his wife Sandra. This chip shop is also popular with the cast of the BBC1 drama *Merseybeat*, who visit the shop when filming nearby.

Les sells cod, haddock and plaice at his town centre shops – as well as peas, beans, pies, sausages and gravy. His shops open throughout the day, but close in the evenings to reflect what he believes are the changing fish and chip eating habits of his customers. For Les, the perfect chip comes from a Maris Piper potato, which is crisp and light golden on the outside, soft and fluffy inside. And he likes to be able to see the fish through his crispy, wispy batter. He regularly cooks fish lightly battered, or without batter for those with an eye on their health.

Also in the awards is Seniors Fish Bar and restaurant in Blackpool, where the now world-famous Harry Ramsden's opened its first restaurant outside its Yorkshire home. Opened in 2000 on a site where fish and chips have been sold since 1932, Seniors was North West champion and runner-up in the national Fish and Chip Shop of the Year contest in 2002, Seniors, whose 'signature fish' is John Dory, defies those who doubt that fish and chips can grace a gourmet menu. It is not unusual to see plaice, halibut, lemon sole and scampi on offer and, when available, sea bass, ocean perch, turbot, brill and fresh langoustines. Champagne, house wines and export beers provide an alternative to the traditional pot of tea, making the restaurant popular for family celebrations, and even serious business deals.

One of their secrets is the experience of owner Rick Horobin, a fish merchant for 30 years, who buys fresh fish from nearby Fleetwood. He runs the business with his wife and sons. Their batter is the consistency of single cream and their passion and enthusiasm for a perfect plate of fish and chips every time is unmistakable.

The dish has gained regional academic credibility through the work of Professor John K Walton, of the University of Central Lancashire, the author of *Fish and Chips and The British Working Class*. Professor Walton spent two years researching the economic, social and political history of fish and chips for his 200-page book, first published in the early 1990s and reprinted in 2000.

Brewing Up Magic

Tirril Brewery

IF YOU ENJOY BEER – flavoursome traditional draught beer from the cask, that is – you'll find the North West the happiest of hunting grounds. At the latest count, there were 60 breweries, of various shapes, sizes and ambitions, in the region. Assuming each establishment produces half a dozen different beers (and many of them make many more) there's at least one new beer being brewed for every single day of the year. And yet, unless you know where to look, many of these gems will remain hidden.

Most are classified as micro breweries and, as the name suggests, they're small capacity plants. To beer aficionados they're heroes, but they're often shy of advertising and lack mainstream media attention. Many are in the cellars, back rooms, outhouses or stable blocks of pubs, in which case the search is relatively easy – find the brewpub and the beer is on tap.

The landlord of the Church Inn, Saddleworth, near Oldham, discovered and refurbished an old brewhouse beside his pub and now provides what he claims is the cheapest beer in the country. The Wapping Brewery brews up its magic in the cellars and secret smugglers' passageways beneath the Baltic Fleet pub in Liverpool, whilst the Hart Brewery occupies the stables of a wonderful country pub, the Cartford Bridge Inn, at Little Eccleston, near Blackpool.

Some micros are worth seeking out for their locations as well as their beers. The George Wright Brewery, for example, is in a World War Two bomb-proof shelter near Rainford, St Helens. The area has gone back to nature and is teeming with rabbits and pheasants. The beers are pretty good, too – there's one called Cheeky Pheasant. Heywood's Phoenix Brewery is a micro in a macro, taking up one corner of the huge old original brewery that closed years ago.

Most of the micro breed, however, is in obscure nooks and crannies of industrial estates – but they still produce lovingly crafted delicious beers. Occasionally, a micro brews a beer that wins national recognition. The Coniston Brewery's Coniston Bluebird Bitter won the accolade of Champion Beer of Britain at the Campaign for Real Ale's annual beer festival in London in 1998 and has never looked back. Moorhouse's of Burnley (a notch up from a micro – they own seven pubs) have made a habit of winning prestigious awards at both the CAMRA festival and the Brewing Industry International Awards at Burton on Trent. All the company's main beers have won awards and in their latest remarkable triumph, their Pride of Pendle was judged the World Champion Cask Conditioned Ale, at Burton in 2004.

Brewers are an interesting bunch. In most cases, they are men who have decided to make a lifestyle change, brewers downsizing from big companies, home-brewers going up a notch. Early-retired or redundant engineers, teachers, computer experts, journalists, even a retired master mariner have all caught brewing fever. What they have in common is a collective passion to produce the best possible beers from the finest ingredients.

Let there be no mistake – brewing beer is a much more complex and challenging process than making wine. Where does the water come from and how should it be treated? What sort of barley should be used, and how should it be malted? What about hops – how many for flavour and aroma, and which varieties? The yeast – where does it come from and what extra zest does it impart? How long for maturation? There has never been a time when there were so many beautifully-crafted and flavour-packed beers available.

Gordon Brown, Chancellor of the Exchequer, is not known for his generosity in matters fiscal – but he has reduced the duty payable on relatively small production of beer and thus become the brewers' friend. Believe it or not, he was CAMRA's Politician of the Year for 2004. The result has been an upsurge in new micro breweries. That figure of 60 changes almost weekly.

In the midst of all this euphoria for the new, let us not forget the long-established family traditional breweries – John Willie Lees of Middleton, Holts and Hydes in Manchester, Robinsons in Stockport, Jennings of Cockermouth, Thwaites in Blackburn. They all have large tied estates, so that you can find a Lees or a Robinsons pub, for example, and know exactly what you are going to get – a good session bitter, a premium bitter, a mild (an endangered species these days), a strong ale and several seasonal beers as well. These companies have survived because they have moved with the times, but kept their traditions and integrity intact.

You'll need guidance from your local press and from the sources quoted above for the region's many beer festivals throughout the year. There are single pub celebrations, such as Manchester's Smithfield Hotel's Lancashire Beer Festival in November, Lancashire Day and Liverpool's Head of Steam

The North West is a happy hunting ground for beer lovers. Pictured is The Philharmonic, Liverpool.

St George's Day celebrations. You'll find modest but enthusiastically supported town events like the Oktoberfest in Warrington, and Atherton's Bent and Bongs Beer bash. There are also the big occasions, such as the ticket-only Ales from the Crypt, the Liverpool City Festival in February, held in the basement of the Roman Catholic Cathedral.

As you might imagine, the choice at a festival can be quite bewildering, with beers brought in from all over the United Kingdom and sometimes the rest of Europe. Ask for advice and it will be freely given – beer buffs are a convivial and friendly bunch.

Rare Breeds Make a Comeback

THE TAMWORTH TWO – the wild boar piglets who escaped from the abattoir and became the subject of a TV drama – put Britain's rare breeds firmly on the map. Nicknamed Butch and Sundance, the duo evaded capture for several weeks, before being delivered to an animal sanctuary to live happily ever after.

But now many more old fashioned breeds of livestock, left behind in the race to achieve an intensive farming system, are making a comeback, thanks to the Rare Breeds Survival Trust (RBST) charity. More and more discerning diners are now seeking the quality, taste and flavour of meat from breeds whose descriptive names – Gloucestershire Old Spot, Belted Galloway, Whitefaced Woodland – conjure up an image of farm animals from a different era.

There are currently over 70 listed rare breeds (including cattle, pigs, sheep, poultry, goats and horses) which meet the Trust's genetic and numerical standards of classification. The breed has to have been in existence for 40 years, plus six generations, and can be listed by the RBST if there are fewer than a specified number of registered adult females in existence: for cattle 1,500, pigs 1,000 and sheep 3,000.

Although not many of the breeds originated in the North West, farmers, butchers and chefs in the region are increasingly producing, selling and cooking meat from these cherished livestock. At Savin Hill Farm, near Kendal, brother and sister Shaun and Michelle Partington are building a reputation for the taste and quality of their British White Cattle and Middle White Pigs.

The little-known British White, an attractive breed with black muzzle, ears, feet and socks, is one of Britain's oldest breeds of cattle with a history going back 800 years. It claims direct links with the ancient, indigenous wild white cattle of Whalley Abbey, Lancashire, and today produces a tender, marbled beef with a good, mature flavour. While rib on the bone remains a favourite cut, its fans claim that traditionally less expensive cuts are of a higher quality than commercially produced beef.

Middle White pigs, which originated from across the Pennines near Keighley in West Yorkshire, are better known, thanks in part to Antony Worrall Thomson who is patron of their breeders' club. They produce a creamy, slightly sweeter pork, once tasted, never forgotten, as Savin Hill farmers learn from their

Holker Hall

More old fashioned breeds of livestock are making a comeback.

internet customers across the UK. Pork loin and Middle White sausages are particular favourites and all the products are sold through farmers' markets and at speciality food events.

Nigel Haworth, chef patron of the country-house hotel, restaurant and newly-opened pub at Northcote Manor, near Blackburn, Lancashire, is keen to source rare breeds locally. He has already produced speciality pork dishes using Gloucestershire Old Spot, an old breed from the Vale of the River Severn, traditionally kept in orchards, but also reared by a few North West farmers. The resurgence in demand for better flavour, makes the marbled, sweeter, gamier Old Spot popular with chefs and home cooks alike. Nigel is currently researching suitable breeds for planned mutton dishes.

And rare breed pork is even being used to transform the humble pork pie. In Manchester's Whitefield, The Upper Crust Pie Company is using Gloucester Old Spots and Tamworths in a range of very superior pies. Their traditional range of eight pies and one flan start with the Gloucester, a true pork pie which contains coarse-chopped meat, seasoning and nothing more. The Tewkesbury adds apple and mulled wine, the Cheltenham, apricot and stem ginger, with successive pies adding ever more exotic ingredients.

With a long history of hand-raised pie baking, the wholesale company which supplies delicatessens (and the public via internet ordering) is responding to a growing interest in rare breed pork whose origins can be traced back to the farm.

Brian and Jane Clarkson of Butterlands Farm at Wincle, near Macclesfield, Cheshire, rear Old Spots and the Kune Kune (pronounced Cooney Cooney), a small pig recently saved from extinction in New Zealand and first imported to Britain in 1992. The Kunes, which graze on the Clarksons' woodland, produce a sweeter meat, sold along with dry-cured bacon and sausages and some Longhorn beef at the local market and at the farm shop known as Organic on the Hill.

Higher Crookhey Farm at Cockerham, near Lancaster, rears belted Galloway cattle, traditionally from South West Scotland, a breed that produce well marbled, excellent quality beef with a silky texture. Even red and rare the beef is tender and juicy.

Farmer Alan Walling sells both his own meat, and other regional rare breed products, at farmers' markets and from the butcher's shop on the farm. They include Norfolk Horn lamb, which produces a lean, darker meat, well flavoured and succulent, reared by his business partner David Walton at Longton, near Preston.

For those who have yet to taste rare breed meat, one breeder's epithet gives food for thought: in the future, you won't tell your friends you had lamb or pork for dinner, but Norfolk Horn or Middle White – just as you'd say you were wearing Nike trainers or an Adidas shirt.

Smoking and Curing

SMOKED FOODS – mainly meat, poultry and fish have been enjoyed since antiquity. Foods were salted to preserve them, then hung in huts and caves where smoke from the cooking fires would have pervaded the fish or meat. It is not known who first realised that smoked food was tastier and remained edible for longer, but the practice was widespread. The Romans smoked cheese over apple wood to produce colour and flavour and both the ancient Greeks and Romans smoked fish. Legend has it that the first York hams were smoked over the sawdust of oak trees used to build York Minster.

The smoking process involves first curing by dry salting, brining or marinating (according to the producer), then air-drying the food before smoking. The cure is a major factor in the flavour of the finished product and many producers have their own particular curing recipes, which may include herbs, spices, brown sugar, cider and molasses. The tarry substances in wood smoke kill bacteria and form an impervious layer on the surface of the food, sealing it from the air. The smoke also penetrates the food to impart the characteristic rich, smoky flavour.

At the Port of Lancaster Smokehouse there is a mouth watering range of smoked fish, cheese, poultry and meats.

The choice of wood for smoking also greatly contributes to the taste of the finished product. Oak, beech, hickory and maple are the most popular; sometimes a small amount of aromatic wood such as juniper is added near the end of the smoking process for an extra special flavour.

There are two types of smoking – cold and hot. Some foods such as salmon or trout may be hot or cold smoked. Cold smoking is done in a kiln or smokehouse at a temperature below 30°C (ideally at 25°C) to avoid cooking the food, but which allows the food to change in colour, flavour and texture. Cold smoked foods include kippers and bacon. Hot smoking is carried out at a temperature of 70-80°C and sometimes higher, in order to cook the food. Hot smoked foods include duck and chicken.

Many large-scale commercially smoked foods are produced in high volume smoking factories, with less smoking time than the traditional product (to reduce weight loss) and the use of dyes to simulate the appearance of a product smoked for a longer period. Unfortunately such products are often accepted as the norm and many people (especially in the case of supermarket smoked salmon), have never tasted the full-flavoured traditional product.

Curing and smoking is a skilled art and takes years to perfect. The combination of top quality fresh foods, smoked using time-honoured methods, results in succulent products with an exquisite and memorable flavour. The North West has a number of traditional smokers, each producing foods with their own distinctive flavour.

Bessy Beck Trout Farm is chemical free and is spring-fed from the source of the River Lune. The trout are not intensively reared and it takes from 18 months to two years to bring the fish to table size. The farm also has two fly fishing lakes, set in beautiful surroundings. Their flavoursome smoked trout fillets are superb.

The Old Smokehouse in Penrith uses local produce in unique recipes of herbs and spices before cold smoking or smoke roasting over oak. Their award-winning smoked Gressingham duck breasts have very little fat and are meltingly tender. They also offer velvety boneless smoked goose breasts and hot and cold smoked venison among their stunning selection of smoked meats, poultry, game and fish.

The Port of Lancaster Smokehouse is situated on the estuary of the River Lune and in season offers River Lune wild salmon and sea trout. Where possible foods are sourced locally and their smoked haddock recently won a prestigious award from North West Fine Foods. Their mouth-watering range of smoked fish, cheese, poultry and meats, includes smoked Lancashire cheese with garlic and black pudding smoked over oak and beech wood. They also offer a smoking service and will smoke products supplied by the customer. If you enjoy fishing and are lucky enough to land a salmon, they will gladly smoke your catch.

Organics Route to Healthy Eating

IT IS HARD TO BELIEVE that it was only around 20 years ago that organics were confined mainly to health food shops and thought of as food only to be eaten by strange hippy types. Now you can enter any major retailer and find an abundance of organic produce and this revolution is growing, with £1 billion spent on produce in 2003, and the North West is a part of it, with 161 organic farms now in the region. In fact, sales of organics have gone up tenfold in the past ten years.

Howbarrow Organic Farm

Howbarrow Organic Farm, where an extensive range of vegetables, herbs and fruit is grown.

But just what is organic? Organic farming means farming with natural, rather than man-made, fertilisers and pesticides. Farmers rely on various techniques, such as crop rotation and the use of resistant varieties to compensate for the absence of chemicals. Animals kept on organic farms are reared according to rigorous animal welfare standards and given a diet of natural feed, which does not contain genetically modified products. The animals are kept in such a way that they can express their natural behaviour as much as possible. Also the routine use of antibiotics is prohibited under organic regulations.

Many people who buy organic say they do so because they believe it tastes better or they feel that food not treated with pesticides is just safer. However, simply buying organic cannot guarantee you freshness and quality, as the produce could have already flown thousands of miles, increasing the price and damaging the environment through food miles.

We still import more than half of our organic food, which seems a shame as by buying good, seasonal produce from local farm shops and box schemes you know it will be fresh and you can check its traceability and quality. There are award-winning shops and producers throughout the North West with a passion for organics.

Mehr Fadoonji learnt her trade on the Ghandi land-gift project in India. Since 1962 she has run Oakcroft Organic Gardens in Malpas, Cheshire, growing a small but steady amount of organic fruit and vegetables which she sells at farmers' markets across the region and also through local box deliveries.

City dwellers can get their organic food delivered straight to their door through box schemes run by companies such as Organic Direct in Liverpool or they can head to the Unicorn Grocery in south Manchester. This co-operative, which opened in 1996, is owned and run by its workforce and it has become one of the largest whole food outlets in the North West, offering between 30 to 70 lines of organic fruit and vegetables. Produce is bought locally and seasonally where possible and sold at reasonable prices. If necessary, stock is imported directly from Europe to ensure quality.

Wirral-based Church Farm Organics, which was voted Organic Farm Shop of the Year 2004 by the Soil Association, also offers local deliveries. Owner Steve Ledsham is proud of the fact that around 83 per cent of the vegetables he sells at the shop are grown on his own small farm and visitors to the shop can pick up everything from organic ice cream to toothpaste.

Similar box schemes and farm shops can be found all over the North West and places such as the Soil Association website www.soilassociation.org can help you find your nearest stockist. If you seek beef and lamb with real taste then visit Forster's at St Helens. Their conversion to organic was at first a commercial decision but they quickly realised how much healthier and happier their animals were and how much better their meat tasted. Chris Forster trained as a butcher so he is able to make sure that they can provide complete traceability and service from the land to the customer.

Within the Peak District National Park you will find Organic on the Hill, an organic livestock hill farm producing home-reared beef, lamb and pork. After 23 years of farming using modern techniques, Brian and Jane Clarkson realised they were dissatisfied with this way of life and wanted to return to a more natural and sustainable way of farming, so they turned organic.

For organic herbs, there's McKinsey's Healthy Herbs near Wigan. Mandy Wellens-Bray caught the organics bug at agricultural college and has developed a huge range of varieties at her nursery, which now also has a small tearoom.

Bob Kitching had been making cheese for 30 years and always wanted his own business, so when the chance came to convert some old farm buildings at Leagram Hall Estate in Lancashire, he grabbed the opportunity. The decision to produce only organic cheese was the result of wanting to support local farmers, but it has also provided a unique selling point. In its first year, 2001, Leagram Organic Dairy won a Gold at the British Cheese Awards. They now have 23 varieties ranging from a traditional Lancashire and Wensleydale to a soft Lancashire and a hard sheep's cheese.

Tip To totally immerse yourself in the organic experience, some farms offer organic bed and breakfast and holidays. www.organic-holidays.com lists 20 such places to stay in the North West, mostly in the Lake District.
One of these is Howbarrow Organic Farm in Cartmel. Voted UK Organic Farm Shop of the Year 2002, Paul Hughes and Julia Sayburn grow an extensive range of vegetables, herbs and fruit, which they sell through their shop and a local box scheme. Their mixed salad won an award for excellence at the North West Producer of the Year 2003 Awards, run by North West Fine Foods. They also breed and raise their own livestock.

These producers are just some of the growing number helping the organic movement in the North West to flourish. Seek them out whenever you can and you will be guaranteed a friendly welcome, enthusiasm and the chance to see exactly how your food is produced. Not only that but you will be assured of getting the freshest and the best tasting available.

For more information visit www.nworganiccentre.org

Farmers' Markets Widen Choice

THE MAIN COMPLAINT ABOUT FARMERS' MARKETS is that shoppers always come back with far more items than they ever intended to buy. But that's what food shopping should be about: being tempted by an unexpected bunch of just-cut asparagus; asking the farmer which is the best way to cook a joint of richly marbled, rare-breed beef; deciding to buy that jar of freshly made lemon curd. It's about talking to the man or woman who grows, rears, catches, brews, picks, pickles, bakes or smokes the food on your table.

Farmers' markets are about bringing people together who have lost touch with each other. It's about more than cutting out the middleman; it's about demonstrating that how you shop directly affects your local environment. It's about communication between farmer and consumer, finding out about where

NWFF

Farmers' markets like this one at Ashton under Lyne provide good social banter.

your food comes from, supporting local enterprise and agricultural diversity, cutting down on food miles and unnecessary packaging, and keeping money in the local economy. It's about local food, seasonal food, fresh food and frequently also about cheaper food. In less than ten years (the first fledgling market in Britain started in 1997) the growth of farmers' markets has been nothing less than phenomenal.

The concept of farmers' markets is, of course, as old as agriculture itself, but today's movement is not about turning back the clock. Nor is it about boycotting supermarkets, but rather about choice and alternative ways of shopping. It's also about having a good day out and in the North West there's a packed calendar to choose from. You can visit a farmers' market practically every week of the year: once you get the habit, there's no going back.

The shire counties are richly endowed with farmers' markets as befits their rural image. Lancashire boasts fifteen, Cumbria at least a dozen and Cheshire

Food festivals add an enjoyable dimension to the shopping experience.

eleven. Urbanites in the two major conurbations are also well catered for with growers and producers offering fresh produce at seven locations in Greater Manchester and five on Merseyside.

All markets have their own specialities and characters. A legend in his own hill farm, Peter Gott of Sillfield Farm in Cumbria became a frequent and popular sight, attired in bowler hat, plus fours, kerchief and braces. His wild boar and sausages needed no hard sell; you could always spot him by the queues thronging his stall. No longer involved in markets, he still participates in shows.

At Eddisbury farmers' market, in Vale Royal, no one can go away without a couple of bottles of juice pressed from some of the 26 varieties of apple grown on the farm where the market is held. The Merchant of Hoghton farmers' market is held in the splendid seventh century setting of the Great Barn at Hoghton Tower, whilst that of Orton in Cumbria fills the streets of this pretty moorland village. Orton, in fact, was the first in the UK to receive accreditation from the National Association of Farmers' Markets and now boasts over 40 stalls selling everything from farmhouse cheese and butter to organic breads and chickens.

Manchester's market is in the middle of the city centre, ironically close by the site of the old wholesale market; Knutsford's is just off the main street, and is brilliant for eggs and smoked trout. The Nantwich farmers' market has strong links with the Crewe and Nantwich Sustainability Alliance, which addresses environmental issues in that borough. In other words, shopping at farmers' markets is less about financial transactions, and more about linking in with a community who care about food and who are out to celebrate its pleasures.

Six months of each year sees a food festival of one sort or another somewhere in the region. Westmorland and Tatton Park, in June and October respectively, are the highlights of the year but Chester, Manchester, Liverpool, Cumbria and Northwich all boast their own events, and well-established social occasions, such as the Cheshire and Royal Lancashire Shows, the Lowther Driving Trials and the Southport Flower Show, invariably host their own food sections. The annual Nantwich Food and Drink Festival which takes place in the last weekend of September, is like many of these increasingly popular food festivals: it is designed to inspire food lovers, and has evolved from a local food fair into a celebration of all that is great about regional produce.

For further information on events listings and farmers' markets go to www.nwff.co.uk and www.nwfantasticfoods.co.uk

Innovation in the Food Hall

HISTORY DOES NOT RELATE WHETHER, IN 1847, the 19-year-old Blackpool tea dealer Edwin Henry Booth read the story of his future success in the leaves but, five generations on, his entrepreneurial spirit continues to guide Britain's leading regional supermarket. Edwin's philosophy was simple and remarkably contemporary: 'to sell the best goods available in attractive stores staffed with first class assistants.'

From his first small shop, The China House, he soon expanded with new outlets selling groceries, Italian delicacies, wines and spirits. In 1859, when the

Booths make a virtue out of selling and promoting regional produce.

Preston store opened, with characteristic marketing flair he gave away free teapots to all customers buying tea. The company had started as it meant to go on.

After the First World War, they expanded further, and by the 1950s there were 14 stores in the chain. At this time, a significant, and typically far-sighted, decision was made to convert the shops to self-service supermarkets. At the time, this was a radical approach to retailing outside London, but Booths have grown steadily ever since, and now have 25 stores stretching from Keswick to Knutsford, and from Poulton to Settle.

Nonetheless, they have firmly kept both their traditional, core beliefs in innovative service, product quality and staff retention, as well as a loyal customer base. For many of the latter, Booths remains far less an impersonal multiple than simply a large, friendly family store or good food emporium, occupying a comfortable middle ground somewhere between an anonymous supermarket and a department store food hall.

Rooted in – and identifying with – the region, Booths has always had a clear idea of the vital role a large retailer must play in the community, and is noted for its long-term support and promotion of regional produce. Around 25 per cent of their goods are sourced from local growers and suppliers, a level virtually unmatched elsewhere in the country. It may seem a given, but at the

Booths' excellent own-label tea and coffee remains a cornerstone of the business.

time it was an act of faith for Booths to fly the North West flag, when the rest of the supermarket industry was blindly driven by the engine of price and the logistics of central purchasing.

That vision has paid off, and in recent years their sales growth has exceeded that of the industry as a whole. This achievement has been underlined by a number of awards, including BBC Radio 4's Food and Farming Awards for Best National and Regional Retailer in 2003. Even the Prince of Wales has expressed his admiration of the firm's achievements.

Booths' commitment to regional food manifests itself in various ways: they sponsor, for example, the hotly contested North West Producer of the Year Competition, run by North West Fine Foods, which is of considerable commercial importance to the winners. In store, at competitive prices, there are products such as Farmhouse Fare puddings, Waberthwaite Cumberland sausages and Morecambe Bay potted shrimps from Furness Fish, Poultry and Game, who cite the company's local sourcing policy as a key ingredient in their success.

Bowland fresh milk, collected from only 15 specially selected farms in the Forest of Bowland, and bottled at a dedicated local centre, is the result of an initiative originally put forward by the farmers themselves, which enables them to receive a higher premium for their milk than they would otherwise obtain on the commercial market. Behind the scenes, this strong relationship with local suppliers not only helps them work together to develop new products, but ensures goods are always delivered tip-top fresh and in perfect condition.

Excellent own-label tea and coffee remains a cornerstone of the business. Coffee is roasted daily under the supervision of resident coffee guru Brian Jackson, then rushed out to the stores where, next day, customers can grind the beans to their own specifications. Wines, now available on-line, are also one of the company's strengths, featuring many distinctive and imaginative bottles from the sort of small, individual grower often squeezed out by the big producer. Regional has never meant fusty provincialism, and Booths' innovative, pre-order 'By Request' service, launched in 2003, has given customers the opportunity to enjoy a range of specialist products unique in the supermarket industry: suckling pig, cooked lobster, whole turbot, banana leaves, salsify, samphire, Sicilian lemons, smoked garlic, guava, quince and Perigord truffles are amongst the 40 or so fabulous products available.

Innovation, too, is nothing new. Back in 1902, John Booth capitalised on a trend of the day with the launch of in-store cafés, a tradition carried on still in many of their stores. The concept, however, had a twenty-first century makeover with the opening of the new state-of-the-art Kendal store which includes, not only a specialist, seasonal farm shop, but a slate and oak restaurant with a menu designed by Steven Doherty of The Punch Bowl Inn, Crosthwaite showcasing Cumbrian produce. Eat the food, then buy it. It's a great idea.

www.booths-supermarkets.co.uk

Chefs Serve Up a Food Renaissance

IN THE EARLY 1990s North West chefs began pushing in earnest for regional produce to feature on North West restaurant menus. The pioneers were the Ribble Valley duo of Paul Heathcote and Nigel Haworth, who badgered North West farmers and food producers to put the flavour back in food. Within a couple of years the regionality movement in both menus and produce among North West chefs quickly spread far beyond the Ribble Valley until it extended from Cheshire to Cumbria.

In a business where traditionally there is commercial and status rivalry in

Chris Tofalos

Steven Doherty with the North West Young Chef of the Year 2004, Martin Holmes.

sourcing, promoting and acquiring better regional food, North West chefs united to focus the region's artisan producers to recognise that restaurants were an untapped market. Recipes may remain secret, but North West chefs now have an open kitchen door to each other as to where the best regional produce can be found.

Nick Foster's passion for sourcing top quality produce from the Lake District rivals his passion for cooking. In the seven years he has been head chef at the Drunken Duck Inn, midway between Ambleside and Hawkshead, he has developed the inn's reputation as one of the serious destination restaurants in the Lake District.

It was always a frustration for Nick that he could see sheep on the hills and cattle in the valleys of Cumbria, yet be unable to get hold of either for the restaurant. The problem lay in the lack of a supply chain from local farm to local kitchen.

Herdwick lamb is the biggest selling item of Cumbrian fresh produce on the Drunken Duck menu. It comes from the nearby Langdale Valley and Nick describes it as slightly stronger in flavour than other more anonymous lamb, whilst also being less fatty, probably due to the rigours of life on the Cumbrian fells.

Nick is a big supporter of Cumbrian food producers, but is always pushing them for more provenance, so he can tell customers not just that ingredients are Cumbria produced, but also from which farm in Cumbria.

As owner of one of Liverpool's best-known restaurants, Gary Manning and his kitchen team at 60 Hope Street have to balance any desire to source high quality North West ingredients with the assurance that the service levels of suppliers are always consistent. When the restaurant opened five years ago neither speciality food producers nor farmers were interested in the restaurant business. Despite West Lancashire and Merseyside having hundreds of acres under cultivation, production was often geared to volume at the expense of taste.

Gary believes that situation is changing and specialist growers have realised that tomatoes grown for their rich flavour rather than just 'red, round and six to the pound', earn better profit. This movement by North West growers is not just rejuvenating traditional North West produce. Vegetables such as speciality salad leaves, which restaurants like 60 Hope Street demand, are now under cultivation in West Lancashire instead of having to be imported from France, Holland or Spain.

It is not just vegetables that are sourced regionally at 60 Hope Street. Almost all the cheeses come from Cheshire or Lancashire, with the only foreign cheese ever appearing on the cheese board being the occasional speciality Irish cheese. Batter for fish and chips is made using beer from Cains brewery close to the Albert Dock; bacon is traditional dry-cured from Cheshire and lamb comes from the salt marshes of the River Ribble estuary.

Yet the most surprising local produce in constant demand at 60 Hope Street is Formby asparagus, the best he has ever tasted, according to Gary. Originally grown to supply grand passenger liners docking at Liverpool in the early twentieth century, it is being served once again on local restaurant tables.

Craig Wilkinson has been at the Bay Horse Inn at Forton near Lancaster for twelve years and has always sourced as much produce as possible from the North West. What has changed is that Craig now tells customers about it. Lamb comes from the Forest of Bowland, beef from the Cumbrian Fell Bred marketing scheme and corn-fed chicken from Goosnargh Village.

One of the best selling items on the menu combines two famous local ingredients, Bowland lamb shank, slow braised in Lancaster Bomber ale. The Bay Horse dish of Flookburgh potted shrimps with chives and brandy is such a popular starter that the pub now sells them in sealed jars for customers to take home.

Cheese features both on the bar snack menu for sandwiches and ploughman's lunches, as well as in the restaurant and almost all are Lancashire produced. From rich blues to mild and creamy, Craig has no reason to look any further than Lancashire for excellent cheese.

Menus at The Bay Horse Inn, Forton, regularly feature local produce.

Such is the passion for local produce at the Bay Horse, that rather than buying imported dried garlic, the chefs go to the nearby fast-flowing River Cocker and gather fresh wild garlic. Another very traditional North West food – samphire – comes from the banks of the River Wyre, and is gathered by the Fleetwood fish merchant whom the Bay Horse uses.

One of the region's most original chefs is Simon Rogan, chef-proprietor of L'Enclume, the executive restaurant with rooms in the Cumbrian village of Cartmel. His innovative menus have been attracting comment not just in the North West, but throughout Britain.

His dishes are on the leading edge of culinary development, bringing new ingredient combinations, cookery and presentation methods. Yet while cubism in foie gras with liquorice and Sichuan syrup might sound like a starter with ingredients from around the world, Simon is passionate about using as much local produce as possible.

All his red meat comes from South Cumbria, chosen for its wonderful flavour. Many of the vegetables are grown at a nearby organic farm, wild mushrooms are sourced from the ancient woodlands in the Lake District, while traditional but neglected herbs such as bergamot, woodruffe, mountain sorrel and coltsfoot are gathered from the wild.

Chefs have become very proactive in promoting North West speciality foods on their menus, but Robert Kisby, executive chef in the Le Mont restaurant in the Urbis Centre in Manchester, thinks there is still more work to be done on both sides.

Suppliers, he argues, need to invest more effort in ensuring continuity of supply and avoid the situation of having to tell a kitchen that production has run out. In turn, chefs also need to show more integrity when dealing with smaller regional suppliers, by not switching at a moment's notice if another supplier offers a similar product a few pence a kilo cheaper.

Speciality regional produce can often be dearer than mass-produced ingredients, but typical of the way chefs can get around this is in the Le Mont menu favourite of Forest of Bowland lamb served with a garnish of Lancashire hotpot. The best end of the lamb goes centre of plate while the off-cuts go into the hotpot garnish.

The key to getting more local speciality foods into North West restaurants is, says Robert, through partnership and commitment on all sides. That way, suppliers, chefs and restaurant customers all stand to benefit.

Formby asparagus is being served once again on Merseyside restaurant tables.

Nigel Haworth
Northcote Manor

NIGEL HAWORTH, AWARD-WINNING CHEF and co-owner of Michelin-starred Northcote Manor at Langho in the Ribble Valley, studied in Switzerland and in leading hotels and restaurants in the UK, before coming back to his roots in Lancashire with his long standing business partner Craig Bancroft, to found one of Lancashire's best known restaurants with rooms. He is a passionate supporter of North West produce and regional dishes form a strong part of the menu mix in the restaurant. His view is that restaurant customers want to taste the dishes they grew up with, but given a modern and lighter touch.

While the ingredients for a North West traditional dish can be sourced almost globally, it is Nigel's view that it borders on deceit to cook a Lancashire hotpot with overseas lamb, Hindle Wakes chicken not using Lancashire-bred chicken, or the wonderful supper dish of baked cheese and egg with a cheese not from the North West.

Yet while Nigel has a commitment to regionally-sourced ingredients, he will not allow Red Rose patriotism to cause him to use anything but the best of ingredients. His kitchen needs the best and Nigel Haworth North West ingredients deliver what he needs. They are, says Nigel – simply the best.

Below is a three course meal created by Nigel using selected ingredients from across the North West.

i   **Northcote Manor**
Northcote Road, Langho, Blackburn BB6 8BE
01254 240 555 www.northcotemanor.com

Northcote Manor

58

Black Pudding and Pink Trout with Onion Rings in Mustard and Nettle Sauce

Northcote Manor

Serves 4

What you need

350g good quality ready-made black pudding mix
200g trout fillet, skinned and pin boned
100g chopped onion

40g butter
12 blanched and chopped nettle leaves or the equivalent in watercress leaves
16 finely sliced onion rings

125g butter for poaching the trout
Juice of 1/4 lemon

400ml chicken stock
150ml white wine
200ml double cream
12 blanched nettle leaves or watercress
Colman's English mustard to taste

What you do

Mustard and Nettle Sauce
Reduce chicken stock and wine by half, add cream and reduce by half again.
Add mustard, liquidise.

Correct seasoning.

Roughly chop the nettles and add before serving.

Deep Fried Onion Rings
Dip the onion ring in milk, pass through a 50/50 mix of paprika and
seasoned plain flour.

Deep fry at 140°C until golden brown.

Black Pudding and Pink Trout
Take a medium stainless steel bowl, place in the black pudding and break
down with the back of a wooden spoon.

Sauté the onions in butter for 30 seconds, place into the pudding mix, season
with salt and pepper.

Line the four moulds with cling film, leaving a good overlap. Divide the
pudding mix equally between the moulds, cover with cling film and press
down well. Steam for 10-12 minutes.

Melt the butter in a medium size heavy bottom pan, place the trout fillets in
and gently poach. In this instance the pan must be covered with a lid to allow
the trout to gently poach in the butter.

Drain off most of the excess butter, add salt, lemon juice and the chopped
nettle leaves, with the back of a fork, flake the trout, until a paté-like
consistency. Check the seasoning and keep warm.

To present the dish

Place the black puddings on to warm plates and take the moulds off.

Divide the trout into four in the pan and quenelle the trout and place on top
(to quenelle, use two spoons to make an oval shape).

Sauce around the black pudding and place the fried onions on top.

Serve quickly.

Lancashire Hotpot

Northcote Manor

What you need

1kg under shoulder, neck and shin of lamb (cut in to 3-4cm thick pieces)
700g thinly sliced onions
1kg peeled King Edward potatoes
25g plain flour
40g salted butter, melted
150ml chicken stock
2tsp sea salt
White pepper

Lancashire Hotpot

What you do

Season the lamb with 1tsp of salt and a good pinch of pepper, dust with the flour. Put the lamb into the base of the hotpot dish.

Sweat off the onions in 15g of butter with 1tsp of salt for 4-5mins (to sweat is to cook without colour in a covered pan, on a moderate to hot temperature). Spread the onions evenly on top of the lamb in the hotpot dish.

Slice the potatoes horizontally (2mm thick). Place in a medium size bowl, add the remaining 25g melted butter, season with 1tsp of salt and a pinch of white pepper, mix well. Put the sliced potatoes evenly on top of the onions, reserving the best shaped rounds for the final layer.

Place the hotpot, covered in a pre-heated oven for 30 minutes on 180-200°C then for approximately 2 hours on 130°C.

Remove from the oven, take off the lid or cover, return to the oven on 180-200°C for 30-40 minutes or until golden brown.

Serve with pickled red cabbage.

Pickled Red Cabbage

What you need

1 head of red cabbage
2 star anise
400ml red wine
275ml malt vinegar
140ml white wine vinegar
140ml balsamic vinegar
5 bay leaves
10 whole cloves
1tsp whole black peppercorns
1tsp whole pink peppercorns
1 stick cinnamon snapped in half
5 whole dried red chillies
12oz caster sugar
55g coarse sea salt for salting the cabbage

Northcote Manor

What you do

Halve and quarter the red cabbage.

De-vein away the large stem and finely slice the red cabbage leaves (alternatively put through a food processor).

Salt the red cabbage well in a colander for 2-3 hours until a deep rich colour is achieved. Drain and wash all the salt away thoroughly – pat dry.

Place all the vinegars, wine and sugar in a suitable pan and reduce by half.

Place all the dry ingredients in a pestle and mortar and coarsely pound.

When the reduction is near completion throw all the dry spices into the reduction and allow to infuse for 5 minutes.

Pass the reduction through a fine sieve and while warm pour on to the red cabbage.

Place the cabbage in a suitable jar and seal, the liquor should just cover the cabbage (store for at least a day).

Apple Crumble Soufflé with Cheshire Ice Cream and Apple Compote

Northcote Manor

What you need

Purée
4 bramley apples
2tbsp potato flour (mixed with a little water to a paste)
80g caster sugar

Soufflé
4 egg whites
4tsp caster sugar

Crumble
150g plain flour
100g butter diced
100g caster sugar

What you do

Apple Purée
Peel, core and slice the apples. Cook on top of the stove until soft.
Allow to cool slightly, then blitz in a liquidiser.
Thicken on the stove with the potato flour paste.
Pass through sieve, cover and refrigerate.

Apple Compote
Peel, core, and dice Granny Smith apples. Bring to boil in water, seasoned
with sugar and lemon juice in a saucepan.
Take off heat and allow to cool in liquid.
Cool and refrigerate.

Apple Baskets
Peel, core and slice the apples across the core on a mandolin, set to 1mm.
Place on silpat or greaseproof paper. Sprinkle with caster sugar.
Bake at approximately 150°C until golden brown.
Allow to cool slightly, then place the apple slices in a dariole mould,
overlapping as you go. The mould should take five rings.
Allow them to set, remove from mould and store in an airtight container.

Crumble Topping
Rub together the flour and butter and add the sugar.
Place on a tray and bake for 15 minutes on 180°C. Allow to cool, breaking
into a crumble and store in an airtight container.

To present the dish

Pre-heat the oven to 185°C. Place the egg whites into a bowl and whisk.
When the whites begin to whisk up, add 4tsp of caster sugar, and whisk until
just before peaks begin to form.

Place 1tbsp of apple purée into a bowl and mix in about 1/3 of the egg
white, then carefully fold in the rest. Place the mixture into soufflé moulds or
ramekins that have been twice buttered and lined with sugar. Gently tap the
base of the mould on the back of your hand, and clean around the edge of
the mould with your thumb.

Bake the soufflé for approximately seven minutes, sprinkle with crumble. Dust
with icing sugar and serve immediately.

Dust the plate with icing sugar over the apple template, then gently tap cocoa
powder over the top.

Place 1tbsp of apple compote into a sorbet pot. Stick the apple basket down
with a little whipped cream, and place a large scoop of Cheshire ice cream
into it.

CUMBRIA

Visitors who flock to Cumbria by the million to enjoy its scenic and man-made attractions are finding a new dimension to its character – that of fine food.

CUMBRIA

IT'S A LANDSCAPE THAT CAN MAKE SPIRITS SOAR, a corner of England that has moved poets, painters and writers, challenged climbers and walkers and charmed tourists and travellers alike. Cumbria is the county of William Wordsworth, John Ruskin, Robert Southey, Beatrix Potter, Arthur Ransome and Norman Nicholson, a place where the stillness of the lakes and the rich tapestry of farm and fell have been the inspiration for so many lives and livelihoods.

Visitors who flock to Cumbria by the million to enjoy its scenic and man-made attractions are finding a new dimension to its character – that of fine food. Alongside its established reputation for quality restaurants, elegant hotels and welcoming pubs, is the growing excellence of locally produced food and drink.

Farmers, growers and artisan craftsmen have emerged from the dark shadow of the 2001 Foot and Mouth crisis with new optimism, new products, new ideas and a new determination to get closer to the consumer.

Towns and villages are peppered with farm shops, food halls and farmers' markets offering easy access to a dazzling range of home-produced fresh meats, pies, dairy foods, vegetables, preserves, artisan breads and confectionery.

The link between food and tourism is at its strongest in Cumbria and there's a wealth of information to help visitors plan their food pilgrimage around the county. The Cumbria Tourist Board has produced a free 169-page guide, *The Taste District*, to help people 'discover a whole landscape of food and drink'.

There's also an *Ale Trail* leaflet that is full of interesting detail about Cumbria's 14 local breweries, and where to drink their beers, and a *Damson Trail* guide to local damson producers in the picturesque Lyth Valley. The Cumbria Fells and Dales Leader Programme has published a guide that helps visitors discover the wide variety of apples in the area.

The increased interest in healthy eating has also manifested itself in the emergence of several organic producer networks including Cumbria Organics, which lists 26 places where consumers can find fresh local organic produce. Over 70 producers are now registered as organic in Cumbria. Some farmers have opened up their own trails to give visitors first-hand experience of how organic food is produced and to illustrate the benefits which such methods bestow on the countryside.

One of the biggest concentrations of local food can be found at the two Westmorland farm shops on either side of the M6 at Tebay. Named as Best Food

Retailer in the BBC Radio 4 Food and Farming Awards, their product line runs to 1200 items with over half originating in Cumbria.

Some of the food on sale – which can also be ordered through the website www.westmorland.com – is produced by Gold medal winners at the Great Taste Awards in London, names like Hawkshead Relish, Jeremy's Soups from Appleby, The Old Smokehouse and Truffles, near Penrith, Country Fare at Mallerstang (cakes, puddings, biscuits, pickles) and Demels in Ulverston (pickles).

Small producers are passionate about their produce and the time-honoured way in which it is made. Woodall's of Waberthwaite, an eighth generation business, and Peter Gott of Sillfield Farm have won many admirers for their hams, bacon and sausages – and their championing of local producers. Peter Gott's wild boar prosciutto has been described as 'one of the twenty things you must eat before you die'.

Cumbria has a growing interest in more traditional and specialist breeds of cattle, sheep and pigs, by both the farmer and the consumer. Names like Belted Galloway, Scottish Blackface, Kendal Rough Fell, Herdwicks, Saddleback and Gloucester Old Spot spring from the pages of *The Taste District* publication.

British White cattle and Middle White pigs are the favoured breeds of Michelle and Shaun Partington who run Savin Hall Farm in the Lyth Valley. Michelle feels the animals are part of British farming heritage and should continue. They are slower to mature and less economically viable but the flavour of the beef and pork is a highly marketable commodity. Savin Hill has won Gold at the Great Taste Awards for its Middle White pork sausage and weeks later triumphed as Producer of the Year at the Manchester Food and Drink Festival.

Small producers receive a helping hand on finding new retail outlets from the Made in Cumbria support group which runs a number of farmers' markets and three shops (Forton Services on the M6, Grasmere and Carlisle) under the Food from the Fells and Spirit of Cumbria brands.

Country shows and sports gatherings also provide a useful shop window for many independent producers and many of the county's leading hotels and top chefs such as David McLaughlin of Holbeck Ghyll Country House Hotel make a virtue out of sourcing fresh local produce for their tables.

Sarah Nelson's Grasmere Gingerbread

Sarah Nelson's Grasmere Gingerbread

IF WILLIAM WORDSWORTH HAD LIVED another four years he might well have penned an ode to Sarah Nelson's Grasmere Gingerbread. She started trading in the small Lakeland village of Grasmere in1854 only a short distance from the poet's last home at Rydal Mount.

The gingerbread is one of the famous icons of Cumbrian food, a cross between a biscuit and a cake, chewy in the middle and crumbly on top. Sarah Nelson invented the recipe with a French chef and the result was an immediate hit with villagers and Victorian tourists alike.

One hundred and fifty years later, particularly in summer, queues still form outside the Church Cottage gingerbread shop. Tourists visiting Wordsworth's grave in nearby St Oswald's Church are guided to the shop by the wonderful aroma wafting across the graveyard as the gingerbreads are being baked.

Joanne Wilson who runs the business with her husband Andrew Hunter is the third generation of Wilsons to make this Lakeland speciality. Only three people know the recipe which was initially scrawled on a piece of paper: Andrew, the person who prepares the mixture in the kitchens to that original recipe, and his parents-in-law, Margaret and Gerald. Baking takes place six and often seven days a week.

Customers have included Prince Andrew, Tom Cruise, Nicole Kidman,

Jamie Oliver and Julie Goodyear. In fact, the gingerbread has fans all over the world, particularly in Japan and the United States. It is despatched to places elsewhere in Britain and abroad, wrapped, as it always is, in its distinctive vegetable parchment.

Sarah Nelson, herself, died 100 years ago and is buried just behind the shop that now bears her name.

> *i* **Sarah Nelson's Grasmere Gingerbread**
> **Church Cottage, Grasmere, Ambleside LA22 9SW**
> **015394 35428   www.grasmeregingerbread.co.uk**

Wild And Fruitful

IT WAS THE TASTE OF HER GRANNY'S DAMSON JAM and bramble jelly that first stirred the imagination of Jane Maggs. Forty years later she is making a living and a name for herself as Wild and Fruitful, the producer behind a range of jams, jellies, marmalades, chutneys, relishes, curds and sauces.

Her main aim is to create preserves using locally produced fruit, herbs and vegetables. She either picks or grows the fruit herself or obtains it from other private gardens, farmers, orchards and National Trust properties. Most of the fruit is grown without using artificial sprays or fertilisers and all of it is traceable, sometimes down to a single tree. Exotic fruit, such as citrus, is organically grown where possible. The label of each jar or bottle gives the origin of the main ingredients.

In 2003, Jane was joint supreme champion in the North West Producer of the Year Awards for her Hedgerow Chilli Jelly, made from rosehips, crab apples, hawthorn haws and chilli peppers. Initially her idea was to use it in stir fries but she tried it with cheese one day and thought the combination was great. The same jelly also won her Silver at the Great Taste Awards in London in 2003.

Trained as a landscape architect, Jane hadn't found much call for her profession after moving to Cumbria's Solway coast two years earlier. So she decided to make use of the abundance of damsons, blackberries, sloes, rosehips and rowanberries she came across in the countryside.

She is keen to promote older varieties of fruit but uses both new and old fashioned recipes. As the whole process is pretty small scale she is able to make a huge range of preserves according to the season.

The range includes Strawberry, Camomile and Lavender Jam; Medlar Jelly; Lemon Curd; Green Tomato, Lime and Vanilla Jam; Garlic and Ginger Olive Oil and Gooseberry and Elderflower Jelly, the latter being awarded Silver at the Great Taste Awards of 2003.

> *i* **Wild and Fruitful**
> **Hillside, Cuddy Lonning, Wigton CA7 0AA**
> **016973 44304**
> **clover@maryport1.fsnet.co.uk**
> **www.wildandfruitful.co.uk**

The produce can be bought at Made in Cumbria shops in Carlisle and Grasmere, Rheged near Penrith, National Trust properties in Cumbria, the Holker Food Hall, Forton services on the M6, Ullswater Steamers, Ravenglass and Eskdale Railway and other outlets in Cumbria.

Wild and Fruitful and NWFF

Richard Woodall's Sausages

IN THE YEAR THAT REGENT'S PARK opened in London and the Duke of Wellington became Prime Minister, Hannah Woodall started to cure and process pigs from neighbouring farms to supplement her income. A hundred and twenty-five years later, Richard Woodall joined the family business in the village of Waberthwaite, the seventh generation of his family to be involved. He, his wife June and his nephew Colin (eighth generation) are directors and a niece Joyce also plays an important role in the retail side of the business.

The company specialises in the production of traditionally dry-cured bacon, air-dried ham, Cumberland ham, pancetta and Cumberland sausage. It holds a Royal Warrant for its bacon, hams and sausage. The 97 per cent meat sausage, with no preservatives or colouring, is made to an original recipe and original techniques are still employed in the curing of hams. Traditional dry curing, says Richard, uses salt, sugar and saltpetre only.

For the Cumbria air-dried ham, the meat is rubbed with this mixture, laid

Richard Woodall Ltd

on a bed of salt for a number of weeks, washed, dried and then hung for a minimum of 12 months to mature. Their Cumbria mature royal ham, using a recipe from 1843, is soaked in a rich pickle of ale, molasses and brown sugar and then lightly smoked.

Pigs for the business are bred on a farm belonging to Richard Woodall's brother Joseph and his son Ian, where the family have operated a closed herd of 180 breeding sows since 1976. This means that no outside animals are brought in as replacements, thus minimising the risk of disease being imported on to the farm. No growth promoters or hormones are used on the animals either.

Time, patience and tradition are deeply embedded in this famous Cumbrian producer and Richard believes that quality, service and old fashioned recipes have served them well. Woodall's latest offering is diced pancetta complete with recipe cards and serving suggestions. Such new products, which capture the interest of younger people and those who are looking for real taste in their food, still excite Richard, his passion for the business seemingly every bit as strong as it was in 1953.

i **Richard Woodall Ltd**
Lane End, Waberthwaite, near Millom LA19 5YJ
01229 717237   www.richardwoodall.co.uk

Strawberry Bank Liqueurs

THE MASONS ARMS AT STRAWBERRY BANK, Cartmel Fell, has one of the finest locations of any pub in the Lake District, yet this was the place that Mike and Helen Walsh left behind in 2002 to set up Strawberry Bank Liqueurs.

When Foot and Mouth struck in 2001 the pub went very quiet because so many footpaths were closed to walkers. As damson beer used to be made on the premises, the couple started producing damson gin to give them extra income. It proved so popular that they decided to concentrate on gin production full time. In 2003 they went through three tons of damsons, damson gin (ABV 25 per cent) being more than half of what they produce. The rest is split between Sloe Gin, Blackberry Gin, Strawberry Vodka and a whisky-based blackberry liqueur.

They live in the picturesque Lyth Valley, an area of Cumbria famed for its damsons, so the raw material for one of their products is not difficult to source.

Helen uses fruit from two orchards at the back of her house and buys in fruit from local farmers in September. Milling the whole damsons takes place in the garden and Mike's hands are usually purple for weeks afterwards.

Mixing (only sugar and London Dry Gin are added to the damson juice) and bottling is done in a production unit at the Lakeland Food Park, Plumgarths, near Kendal. From there the drink finds its way into a number of retail outlets including Booths supermarkets, ASDA stores, the Holker Food Hall at Holker Hall, Made in Cumbria shops, the Tatton Park farm shop in Cheshire, and a number of farmers' markets in Cumbria. Helen recommends Blackberry Gin with lemonade or soda water as a 'great long drink for summer'.

i **Strawberry Bank Liqueurs**
Wood Yeat Barn, Crosthwaite, Kendal
015395 68812 or 01539 736192 www.damsongin.com

Holker Food Hall

Holker Hall

EVERY YEAR 60,000 or so annual visitors explore the rose-coloured Victorian mansion, stroll through the 25-acre garden and steer around the Lakeland Motor Museum of the Holker Estate in south Cumbria, home of the Cavendish family. The latest attraction, a food hall, promises the best of produce from the Holker estate, top quality produce from elsewhere in Cumbria and a selection of food and wine from Tuscany where Lord and Lady Cavendish own a property.

The Foot and Mouth outbreak in 2001 provided the impetus for this new venture. Shortly after Cumbria was rid of the epidemic, the estate got together with three of its tenant farmers to discuss marketing local saltmarsh lamb, long considered a delicacy in France. The Holker estate realised that, with animals grazing land on the Cartmel peninsula beside Morecambe Bay, it could ensure that its tenants received a premium price for the lamb, which the estate could then brand and sell on. Thus was born Holker Saltmarsh Lamb, endorsed in 2002 by food writer Clarissa Dickson Wright.

Building on that success led to the creation of the food hall, which sells lamb and beef from the 15,000 acre estate as well as other food and drink that is either processed at Holker or made especially for the estate from elsewhere in Cumbria.

The latter includes bread from the Staff of Life bakery in Kendal, pies from Savin Hill Farm in the Lyth Valley, Flookburgh shrimps, cheese from the Cheese Shop in Kendal, Cowmire Hall damson gin, Think Drink apple juice, Quiggin's Kendal mint cake and Country Fare cakes. Food hall supervisor Peter Mathew is keen to increase the whole range of products and in particular to offer more items from Cumbria producers.

i
Holker Food Hall
Holker Hall, Cark-in-Cartmel,
Near Grange over Sands LA11 7PL
015395 59084 www.holker-hall.co.uk

Greystone House Farm Shop and Tearoom

GREYSTONE FARM IS A WORKING 119-HECTARES FARM that has been in the Dawson family since 1752. When the current owners, John and Marjorie Dawson, lost their entire livestock in the Foot and Mouth outbreak they grasped the opportunity to make a lifestyle change by converting to organic and opening a farm shop and tearoom in a listed oak-beam building formerly used as a general store.

Situated on the edge of the Lake District National Park, the shop opens daily from 10am to 5.30pm and acts as a retail hub for the village of Stainton. It is also well patronised by visitors on the tourist trails to Ullswater just three miles away and to the Rheged Centre nearby.

The shop sells home-reared beef and lamb, organic fruit and vegetables grown on the farm and a veritable banquet of other Cumbria produce including Burbish Pies, Lowther organic chickens, Country Puddings, Thornby Moor cheeses, Hawkshead Relish and Simply Vegetarian meals.

The Dawsons, who have been joined by son Thomas in the business, compete successfully with larger retail outlets by focusing on quality, taste and freshness. There is a traditional butcher's shop and bread and cakes are baked on the premises. The rustic tearoom is located on the shop's upper floor and offers a range of home cooked meals.

Not content with converting to organic farming, the family has also joined the Countryside Stewardship Scheme using payments from DEFRA to establish

two footpaths linking Stainton and Newbiggin, ponds and wildlife strips. The whole venture has quickly made its mark on the locality and in recognition of their enterprise, the Dawsons were given the overall award in the 2003 Countryside Awards, organised by the *Cumberland News*.

i **Greystone House Farm Shop**
Stainton, Penrith CA11 0EF
01768 864 443

Carlisle Farmers' Market

AT THE VERY FIRST CARLISLE FARMERS' MARKET in May 2000, producer Austen Davies took along 220 yards of sausage and sold every inch. Not every market measures up to that first outing but that hasn't deterred him from regular selling sorties at Carlisle on the first Friday of every month.

Although his business, Border County Foods, also produces pork, bacon, hams, black pudding and Cumberland dux (like faggots) and also deals in game, Austen's culinary tour de force is his sausages. Initially, he made them for family and friends but then reached a stage where he was using a whole pig for sausage and, as he says, that's an impressive amount of sausage.

Turning a hobby into a business, he then had to find outlets for his product

and as Carlisle farmers' market was in his 'back garden', Austen signed up from the very first day. He has a tremendously loyal repeat trade although people still find it amusing that he sells his Cumberland sausage by the yard. As a member of the Rare Breeds Survival Trust he keeps pigs like Saddleback, Tamworth, Middle White, Oxford Sandy and Black and the better-known Gloucestershire Old Spot.

Austen is one of about 22 producers who regularly use the Carlisle Market to reach a wider customer base. The market was winner of the Cumberland News' Best Farmers' Market/Farm Shop in 2003. Organised and supported by Made in Cumbria, the market's appeal is the freshness and diversity of local and specialised produce.

Producers who attend include Bromley Green Farm (beef and lamb), Buckles Farm (lamb and pork), Claire's Handmade (preserves and pickles), Country Fare (cakes, puddings, biscuits etc), Cream of Cumbria (butter), Staff of Life (bread), Think Drink (apple juice) and Whiteholme Farm (organic meat).

The market is a well-publicised event in a busy city centre with cookery demonstrations adding to the flavour of the occasion.

i **Carlisle Farmers' Market**
City Centre, Carlisle
01539 732736 www.madeincumbria.co.uk
The market takes place on the first Friday of each month.

Hawkshead Brewery

Hawkshead Brewery

ALEX BRODIE IS A VETERAN JOURNALIST and BBC Radio Foreign Correspondent and served in some of the world's hottest hot spots – including Pakistan, Iran and Israel. When the going got tough, he used to think of cool green Lakeland hills and good traditional English beer. Now, having handed in his flak-jacket, he has made those dreams come true. The Hawkshead Brewery is up and running and doing very well.

You will find the brewery in a beautifully restored seventeenth century barn on the edge of a tiny Quaker settlement – farm, cottages and graveyard – just outside Hawkshead, on the road from the Windermere Ferry. The only clue to its presence is the brewery van, resplendent with livery and logo, parked on a strategic bluff above the road.

The brewery office is plastered with certificates, not just for the beer, which has already won several awards at local beer festivals, but for the restoration work on the barn. In time, there will be a tasting room, but at the moment sampling is done in an open-sided shed, with gate for leaning on and contemplation, plus views of idyllic countryside backed by dreaming fells.

Alex claims to have done half a lifetime's drinking beer and knew what he wanted – friends who were brewers drank with him and explained what to do. Opened in 2003, the brewery now produces draught Hawkshead Bitter and Hawkshead Best, and two bottled beers, Hawkshead Gold and Hawkshead Red – the last two have been taken up by Booths Supermarkets, connoisseurs of good bottled beers, and are available far away from the Lakes. There are plans for a dark mild, a stout and, interestingly, a damson beer – damsons are a speciality crop of south Lakeland.

Hawkshead Brewery
Town End, Hawkshead, Cumbria LA22 0JU
015394 36111

The Queens Head Inn

The Queens Head Inn

OCTOBER 2002 WAS A MONTH TO REMEMBER for Chris Tomlinson, owner of the Queens Head Inn at Tirril near Penrith. Opening the post one morning he came across a letter from the *Good Pub Guide* informing him that his hostelry was once again included in the guide.

A list of national award-winners was also enclosed and as he looked down the various entries, he came across the Queens Head Inn. It was named Pub of the Year 2003, the first he had heard about the award. Flabbergasted, he phoned the *Good Pub Guide* press officer to see if it was a hoax. It wasn't. His secret is simple. He tries to offer his patrons and guests the sort of service he'd want when visiting another pub. That means quality beer, a good selection of wine and whisky (there are over 40 malts), proper home cooked food with fresh produce and a smiling face behind the bar and in the restaurant.

The pub dates from 1719 and flagstones and beams are much in evidence, along with a few hooks for smoking meat that are still in place up the bar chimney. Wine books line a little shelf in the wall.

Once known as The Board, the pub was renamed for the coronation of Queen Victoria in 1838. Two years earlier the property had been bought by John Bewsher from the Wordsworths after it had been in their family for over 20 years.

A copy of the sale document, known locally as the 'Wordsworth Indenture' is displayed in the bar, signed and wax sealed by three Wordsworths, including William, the poet. A best bitter named John Bewsher is also one of five beers that Chris Tomlinson produces at his Tirril Brewery at nearby Brougham Hall.

i **The Queens Head Inn, Tirril, near Penrith CA10 2JF**
01768 863219 www.queensheadinn.co.uk
An annual three day beer and sausage festival is held in August.

Steven Doherty
The Punch Bowl Inn

STEVEN DOHERTY HAS COME BACK TO COOK in the North West of England where he grew up, but his career path has seen him cook in some of the greatest restaurants in Europe. After training in Michelin starred restaurants in France, he took the position of second chef at London's celebrated Le Gavroche restaurant working alongside the legendary Albert Roux. In 1985 he was promoted to head chef of Le Gavroche and became the first British chef to head up a three-starred Michelin restaurant in the UK.

In 1991 Steven and his wife Marjorie moved up to the Lake District and ran the Brown Horse at Winster, where Steven's cooking won national critical praise. In 1995 they moved to the Punch Bowl Inn at Crosthwaite and the accolades followed. Steven's latest challenge has been to set up and run the restaurant operation at one of Britain's biggest kitchen and homeware stores, Lakeland in Windermere, with a determination to show that the skills of a Michelin chef can provide a light lunch or an afternoon tea with the same touch of magic as with a dinner for kings. Below is a dish Steven has chosen using Cumbrian produce.

i **The Punch Bowl Inn**
Crosthwaite, Kendal LA8 8HR
015395 68237 www.punchbowl.fsnet.co.uk

Slow cooked melting rolled Cumbrian-bred belly pork on a grain mustard mash with creamed cabbage and Cumbrian black pudding.

Cumbria Recipe Slow Cooked Melting Rolled Cumbrian-bred Belly Pork on a Grain Mustard Mash with Creamed Cabbage and Cumbrian Black Pudding

Serves 4

What you need

1/2 full side of belly pork, boned, skinned, rolled and tied very tightly. A good local butcher will do this, but ask him to tie it at 1cm intervals.
2 litres duck fat
1 small Savoy cabbage
125ml double cream
500g peeled potatoes (Maris Piper is my recommendation)
150g butter
1 small onion, finely sliced
2tsp grain mustard
1 full head of garlic, peeled but left whole
4 slices of black pudding log
A bay leaf, sprig of thyme, sprig of sage
Salt, pepper, sprinkle of fresh nutmeg

Preparation Time 45 minutes
Cooking Time 2 hours

What you do

Pre-heat the oven to 150°C / 300°F / Gas Mark 3

Melt the duck fat in a deep roasting tray or braising dish and put the pork in the tray, cover with the fat, add the garlic, bay leaf, thyme and sage. Cover with tin foil and cook for 2 hours. Baste occasionally.

Cut the peeled potatoes into 3cm pieces and cook in lightly salted water. Keep them warm.

Finely shred the cabbage, blanch in boiling salted water and drain.

Sweat the onion in a little butter without colour for 15 minutes, add the cream, bring to the boil and lightly season with salt and pepper.

Add the cabbage, mix well, reduce the cream a little more and keep warm.

Prepare the mash, add the remaining butter, mash again and season with salt, pepper and a pinch of nutmeg. Keep warm.

Slice the black pudding, brush with oil and grill.

Remove the pork from the cooking fat and drain on a cooling wire for at least 30 minutes. Cut into 10cm slices then crisp the meat in a hot oven at 220°C / 425°F / Gas Mark 8 for 20 minutes. Remove the string.

To present the dish

Add a little grain mustard to the mash, mix in and arrange into a neat oval in a large pasta bowl or on a large individual plate.

Spoon the cabbage around the mash, put the black pudding on top of the mash and add the pork.

CHEF'S TIPS

- You can prepare the pork a day ahead rolled up in cling film to allow it to cool and firm up in the fridge.

- I like to use duck fat because this enriches the flavour. Regional specialist food shops may sell it and it's available in the regional supermarket Booths, as well as some national supermarket chains. It really is worth hunting out.

- The pork I love to cook with is from the Savin Hill Farm in the Lyth Valley in South Lakeland. They rear the old Middle White breed of pig which is packed with flavour. Savin Hill Farm are regular stallholders at farmers' markets in the North West.

- The Black pudding I use is from RS Ireland in Rossendale. Wonderful black pudding.

LANCASHIRE

Northern food is real food: wholesome, filling and practical. Thrifty Lancastrian housewives instinctively knew how to make a virtue out of simple necessity.

LANCASHIRE

**Gravy and potatoes in a good brown pot,
Bake it in the oven and serve it very hot!**

NORTHERN FOOD IS REAL FOOD: wholesome, filling and practical. Thrifty Lancastrian housewives instinctively knew how to make a virtue out of simple necessity. Lancashire hotpot, for example, is a slow-cooked casserole of lamb chops, kidneys and potatoes, usually served with pickled red cabbage. In Victorian times, it also included oysters, then regarded as the food of the poor. Tripe and onions, too, used to be a cheap, everyday meal, and once every Lancashire town had its own UCP tripe shop. Today the latter may be as rare as the proverbial hen's tooth, but iconic black pudding is alive and well, served steaming hot at Burnley Indoor and Bury Outdoor Markets, or on the plates of modern brasseries from Blackpool to Bolton.

Nonetheless, the traditional food culture of Lancashire has moved on, in the wake of changing tastes and lifestyles. Independent butchers still sell tripe, but it is increasingly difficult to find half-forgotten specialties such as cow-heel, elder (pressed cows' udder), lambs' fry (testicles) and chitterlings (pigs' intestines). Even less arcane delights such as potted meats, salmon paste, faggots and cold pease pudding are becoming rarer: most are as anachronistic as clogs, hairnets and Ena Sharples' famous iced fancies. Even the humble chip 'barm' has been eclipsed by the pizza and pasta generation, although you can still find home cooks who make a nod to heroic tradition with pea and bacon soup, homemade brawn, meat and potato pie, Lancashire 'foots' filled with cheese and bacon, parkin slab and whinberry tart. Thankfully we continue to ignore some fancy southern ways, call our evening meal 'tea' and eat 'dinner' at lunchtime.

The good news, however, is that a number of classic products not only thrive but have achieved national status, particularly Morecambe Bay potted shrimps (though the Southport variety also has its aficionados) and Lancashire cheese, thanks in part to local chefs, such as Paul Heathcote. At Northcote Manor, Nigel Haworth has researched and recreated with modern sensibility recipes such as Hindle Wakes chicken (with leeks and prunes), and eighteenth century Bury black pudding with pink trout and mustard and nettle sauce; at the same time, he uses familiar ingredients in unexpected ways, such as Lancashire cheese ice cream. Little wonder his sensational Lancashire hotpot has become a destination dish that diners drive half way across the country to sample.

Good cooking, however, needs good ingredients, and a new generation of artisan producers and committed farmers has taken the county into the new century with renewed vigour. From the market gardens of the Fylde to the Pennine hill farms, North Sea fishing fleets and industrial heritage towns, the county can boast a choice of great produce from Goosnargh duck and chickens to Mansergh Hall lamb, Pugh's Piglets, Ann Forshaw's yoghurts, Farmhouse Fare puddings, Fairfield Farm gammon steak and a superb range of new blue cheeses, all cornerstones of Lancashire's future food heritage.

At the same time, those products which are uniquely associated with the county such as Bury simnel cake, Chorley cakes, Ormskirk gingerbread and Goosnargh cakes, need both celebration and preservation. Not only products but, in the case of Herbal Health in Rawtenstall, a whole shop, the last surviving Temperance Bar in Britain, still serving Fitzpatrick's original, lip-smackin' brews to the faithful.

Eating with a conscience, however, is something Lancastrians know all about. Rochdale is the world-famous home of the Co-operative Movement; their little store in Toad Lane, opened in 1844, enabled factory workers to afford the basics of daily life. Some 160 years later in Fleetwood, local residents once more started their own co-op, buying food direct from local farmers; so successful has been the scheme, they now have a high street shop. Garstang became the country's first 'Fairtrade' town a few years ago, when the local community agreed to promote food that pays a fair price to farmers in developing countries.

There's more to Red Rose country than meets the eye. Who says we can't knock the skin off a rice pudding?

Lancashire Cheese

CREAMY, CRUMBLY, MILD, TASTY, MATURE, STRONG, organic, unpasteurised, smoked, blue – but always with a distinctive buttery taste, the range of Lancashire cheese is an eye-opener to the uninitiated. It is also one of the best cooking cheeses in the world, especially suitable for toasting as it does not separate on heating. Instead it takes on a silky quality, hence the once-famous Leigh Toaster. When Benn Gunn in Robert Louis Stevenson's *Treasure Island* sighed of the many nights he dreamt of cheese 'toasted mostly', he was probably referring to Lancashire.

Lancashire is one of the oldest territorial cheeses in the country, and retains a strong regional identity, with almost all the farmhouse cheeses produced

Mrs Kirkham's Lancashire Cheese and NWFF

around Preston, Chipping and Garstang. The traditional method is complex and time-consuming, mixing and dividing the curd of consecutive milkings over two to three days, a method unique in the cheese-making world. Avoid industrialised versions, an acid, sharp taste gives the game away. Purists will also avoid spoiling the true taste of Lancashire with novelty 'additives' such as apricot and piccalilli. In order to safeguard the name, reputation and quality, Singleton's have successfully gained the coveted Protected Designation of Origin (PDO) status for their Beacon Fell Traditional Lancashire Cheese. Aged for two months, it is semi-soft in consistency and slightly crumbly, with an even yellow colour and a clean, tangy flavour.

Other excellent examples of Lancashire cheese include Grandma Singleton's in its distinctive red wax, matured for a minimum of nine months and as strong as it comes; Shorrock's unpasteurised, traditional Lancashire with seasonal variations of flavour; the fantastic, young, fresh Creamy and Crumbly Lancashire Organic from Chris Sandham; Butlers Tasty Lancashire; creamy Garstang Blue Lancashire from Dew-Lay, and distinctive Lancashire Blue from Carron Lodge; and anything that comes out of Mrs Kirkham's dairy. Multi award-winning, her unpasteurised Lancashire cheeses are handmade, cloth-wrapped, matured for five to six months and have a marvellous, rounded but delicate flavour. Treasure Island cheeses to dream about every night.

i **Singleton's Dairy Ltd**
Mill Farm, Preston Road, Longridge, Preston PR3 3AN
01772 782112 www.singletons.uk.com

Farmhouse Fare

STICKY TOFFEE PUDDING ORIGINATED at the Sharrow Bay Hotel in Cumbria and has since become arguably the region's (and the nation's) favourite pud. Competing versions are keenly judged, severely marked down for scanty saucing and dry texture, so when outside caterer Helen Colley held a charity coffee morning for Macmillan Nurses in 1998, it was no small accolade when the sticky toffee pudding stall was a complete sell-out.

From this small, sticky step, Helen has built an award-winning company, specialising in puddings, that is 'big enough to cope, small enough to care'. Those who approach their meals backwards and decide on their puddings first,

Farmhouse Fare and NWFF

are likely to face consumer paralysis syndrome when faced with a choice of traditional, 'nursery' varieties such as Sticky Syrup Pudding, Sticky Marmalade and Whiskey, and Sticky Dickie Pudding (with currants, apples and cinnamon toffee sauce). Sticky seems to be the word, but don't overlook the decadent delights of their Chocolate and Orange Pudding, Christmas Pudding Ice Cream and seductive Summer Fruit Pudding with Cassis. You don't even have to go to the bother of turning the pudding into serving dishes with her latest range of fabulous, straight-to-the-table Catalan creams, brulées and puddings sold in glass ramekins and ceramic dishes.

A nominee for the Woman of the Year Award, Helen's key to success has been the way she has combined hand baking methods, small batch production and high quality ingredients, such as real butter and pure orange essence, with modern packaging and production techniques to ensure a rich, moist result, even from the microwave. You'd be proud to pass the results off as your own and, doubtless, many do.

Helen's great-great grandmother Janet Anderson, who features on all the packaging, photographed spinning wool at the family farm, would have been right proud of her and you can't say fairer than that.

 Farmhouse Fare Ltd
Anderson House, Lincoln Way, Salthill, Clitheroe BB7 1QL
01200 453110 www.farmhousefare.co.uk

Black Pudding

RICH AND SPICY BLACK PUDDINGS are a symbol of traditional Lancashire, part of the heritage along with Lowry paintings, brass bands and Victorian warehouses. Unlike other products that have fallen out of fashion, however, black pudding also symbolises new Lancashire. This is thanks in part to regional chefs who have restored it to true gastro-glory using it in modern British dishes such as Andrew Nutter's Crisp Bury Black Pudding Won-tons and Tom Bridge's Bury Black Pudding and Potato with Mustard Sauce.

Black puddings have a long history. Their popularity here is probably due to the concentration of large numbers of urban poor and consequent demand for cheap meat products. Andrew Holt of RS Ireland's The Real Lancashire Black Pudding Company uses a recipe dating back to 1879, and has the original to prove it. Every day the puddings are hand-mixed with a secret combination of 14 herbs and spices, then hand-tied in the traditional Lancashire black pudding fat loops that makes them look like large, shiny castanets when strung together. They are then boiled, cooled and bagged ready for consumption on breakfast tables far and wide.

Andrew makes over half a million black puddings (and 20,000 larger sticks) each year – which is probably enough to circle Bolton's Reebok Stadium several

NWFF

times over. Not only does he have an impressive collection of gongs to hang round his neck (they now have an incredible hundred awards to their credit), but Andrew has also been inaugurated into the select society of the Chevalier du Gout Boudin Noir, which translates as Knight of the Black Pudding. All knights swear an allegiance to the black pudding, promise to promote it wherever and whenever they can, and are touched on the shoulders with a large toasting fork. Vive le Lancashire black pudding! Or as we say in these parts, the proof of the pudding is in the eating.

i **RS Ireland, The Real Lancashire Black Pudding Company**
Pudsville II, Glentop Works, Newchurch Road, Stacksteads,
Bacup, Lancashire OL13 ONH
01706 872172 www.rsireland.co.uk

Sarsaparilla

CORDIAL IS AN EXCELLENT WORD. It defines both a refreshing drink and a proper northern welcome. Mawson's Sarsaparilla Cordial, available in traditional stone bottles, as well as smaller glass ones, harks back in both look and taste to the 1930s, when the firm was originally founded in Oldham.

Made from a combination of herbs including liquorice, ginger and sarsaparilla bark, this lovely, old fashioned drink has an addictive sweet and spicy taste. Herbal brews such as this were once widely enjoyed throughout industrial Lancashire, stronghold of the Temperance Movement, and 'Sass 'n' Soda', diluted with cold fizzy (or still) spring water, remains a refreshing summer drink. It's also excellent mixed with hot water, to warm the cockles of your heart on a frosty Pennine day. The cordial has now been joined by a sparkling version and a lovely, old fashioned cream soda with bubbles that get right up your nose.

The Mawson story began when milkman Joe Mawson bought a herbalist's shop in Oldham. The back room, with its piano, card tables and non-alcoholic beer soon became a popular meeting place, with Joe brewing up to 40 gallons a day in the cellar. When Joe's first opened, there were 36 herbalist's in Oldham, 20 of whom were also temperance bars but, over the years, the numbers dwindled until last orders were called in 1963.

The firm went into the health food and herbs and spices business, but nostalgia called and Joe's son Nigel was prompted to bring back the

NWFF

Sarsaparilla to commemorate the firm's 65th anniversary in 1998. Nigel recalls that for two weeks in August 1998, they gave samples to many old and new customers in the Oldham shop and the first batch of 5,000 bottles sold out in just eight weeks. Since then, the business has grown and Mawson's cordials are available to fans around the country. No one is going to call time on this brew for many years to come.

i **Mawson's Traditional Drinks Ltd**
Unit 11a, Newline Industrial Estate, Bacup OL13 9RW
01706 874 448 www.sarsaparilla.co.uk

Pendle Heritage Centre

PENDLE AND WITCHES GO TOGETHER LIKE TEXTILE AND MILL. The beautiful meadows, moorlands and distinctive profile of Pendle Hill are haunted still by memories of 1612, when eight women and one man were accused of witchcraft. The route they took from their interrogation to their trial and

ultimate hanging at Lancaster can be followed on the Pendle Witches Trail, and the story is also told at the exhibition at Pendle Heritage Centre.

The Heritage Centre is housed in a Grade II listed farmhouse that was home for 300 years to the Bannister family (most notable scion, Sir Roger Bannister of four-minute mile fame). A little oasis of peace after an exhausting trek around the local mill shops, the complex also includes a Gallery and Parlour shop (stock up on local lemon curd!). The Centre is also a perfect starting point for a variety of walks, either a peaceful amble through the eighteenth century walled garden, passing through woodland and the medieval Cruck Barn with its farmyard animals, or the seven mile circular Water Power Trail that links some of the early water-powered sites found beside Pendle Water. Strike out, if you will, along the 45-mile long Pendle Way, or retire gracefully to the Garden Tearoom, overlooking the walled garden, for excellent home cooking and baking, to consider the following interesting snippet of information.

A group of young local men back in the eighteenth century, who were said to be partial to nettle pudding, were frequenters of the nearby Lamb Club, but had a little task to perform before they were allowed to drink there. They had to go out on to the moors to eat the pudding and recite this tongue-twister:

Thimblethwrig and Thistlethwaite,
Who thinking to thrive through thick and thin,
Through throwing thee thimbles hither and thither
Was thwarted and thwacked by thirty three thousand thick thorns.

And that was before even one drink! Amazing what you can learn from a reet good day out in Pendle country.

 Pendle Heritage Centre
Park Hill, Barrowford, near Nelson BB9 6JQ
01282 661702 www.htnw.co.uk

Chilli Lime Deli

MATTHEW MAYMAN IS NEVER HAPPIER than when surrounded by food, and his twin passions for food and travel are reflected in the hand-picked, top quality selection of products lining the shelves and counters of the small, atmospheric shop that would shame many a larger enterprise.

Chilli Lime Deli

The deli is one of six smart shops located in Blackburn's authentically reconstructed Exchange Arcade, built originally in 1849 as the town's first shopping mall, in what used to be the old cotton market. The wallpaper may be William Morris but the products are as contemporary and mouthwatering as you'll find anywhere in the country.

The shop's name derives from the time Matthew lived in Sydney, and is a homage to one of his all-time favourite, down-under dishes: chilli lime crab. Luckily, he has customers to match his own adventurous tastes. Anything with chilli, he notes, sells really well. Chilli jam is one of the deli's top lines. Many of the shop's more unusual products reflect the diverse origin of Matthew's customers, from Thai sauces to Spanish drinking chocolate. An excellent range of spicy pickles with a Southern Indian accent is made locally in Blackburn. And, alongside the Italian pasta flour, Chinese sauces, Australian marinades, French sauces, Welsh sea salt and Scottish flower and herb vinegars, you'll also find some of the North West's best produce, such as Mrs Kirkham's Lancashire cheese, Cartmel Sticky Toffee Pudding and Mawson's Sarsaparilla.

Lunchtime sees a queue of people for ciabatta with Lancashire cheese and pastrami, or 'doorstep' sarnies with salami, or maybe the other way round. Whatever your choice, it's the world on a plate, and you don't even have to leave Blackburn.

 Chilli Lime Deli
17 Fleming Square, Blackburn BB2 2DG
01254 52229 www.chillilimedeli.co.uk

Fairfield Farm Shop

FAIRFIELD IS A PROPER FARM SHOP, in that most of the products sold in the shop come from either the farm itself or from ones nearby. Although they stock local beef and chickens, cheese, freshly laid eggs, home-baked cakes, good chutneys and preserves, the emphasis is on pork products: beautifully trimmed fresh meat, 40 varieties of sausage (including the aptly named Gunk-free), half a dozen cuts of bacon and great joints of ham. When the fabulous gammon won them the 2003 North West Producer of the Year Award, the judges commented on its great texture, wonderful moist flavour and perfect balance of salt and fat.

Fairfield is an unexpected and well-deserved success story. It is particularly remarkable given the shop only opened in 2000 in an attempt to recoup the fortunes of a farm badly hit by the collapse of the pig industry and other agricultural disasters. Although many have attempted such diversification, few have done it with the skill, determination and principles of Philip and Louise Edge. Their reward is a faithful following of loyal customers, including ones who travel many miles to stock up on top quality produce at reasonable prices.

Fairfield's strength is three-fold: traditionally reared pigs housed literally behind the shop; a helpful neighbour who also happens to be one of the country's leading experts in craft butchery; and, last but not least, size. Small is beautiful, and the personal touch that goes with it is all-important.

Philip and Louise have control over every aspect of the farm-to-plate process, and the shop has rapidly expanded to include a smokery, a range of frozen, ready-made dishes, and a farm kitchen serving their own sausages and gammon. They've also achieved a considerable reputation for spectacular presentations: porchetta, joints trimmed in the French style, and beautifully stuffed banquet roasts.

i **Fairfield Farm Shop**
Longsight Road, Clayton le Dale, Blackburn BB2 7JA
01254 812550 www.fairfieldfarm.co.uk

Merchant of Hoghton Farmers' Market

THE MERCHANT OF HOGHTON is not so much a person as a phenomenon. Since it was established in July 2003, the farmers' market has become one of the most popular in the region. Part of the attraction is the setting: the seventeenth century Great Barn at Hoghton Tower must rank as one of the finest anywhere in the country. Just as important, however, is the quality of the produce on offer each month, from fresh fish to meat, bread, jams, olives, cakes and fresh vegetables. About a third of the 40 or so stallholders come from the immediate area, the rest from as far as Cumbria and Wales. It's the smaller producers, however, who are perhaps the most interesting: the individual maker of hand-raised meat pies; the homemade soup seller; the Bury black pudding stand; three Lancashire cheese stalls; producers each specialising in pork, lamb or beef.

Another attraction is the fact the market is under cover, so you don't have to trudge round in the rain trying to stop your paper bag of glossy onions from dissolving in a downpour. Equally, in summer, the grounds of the dramatic fortified hilltop manor house make impromptu picnics on the lawn a pleasure.

The house has been the home of the de Hoghton family since the Norman Conquest, and at 650ft above sea level, the Tower (ie the house) occupies a

commanding position with magnificent views of Lancashire. From July to September visitors to the market (which takes place all year round), have the extra option of a tour of the house and grounds, following in the footsteps of Shakespeare, Dickens and assorted Royal personages.

Allow plenty of time: there is no shortage of attractions at the Market, with carol singers and barrel organs to entertain shoppers in season. And another word of advice – for the cream of the crop, you have to get up early round these parts. Amble in after lunch and you'll be lucky to get a nice, earthy carrot. Just don't tell the regulars we said so.

Merchant of Hoghton Farmers' Market
Hoghton Tower, Hoghton, Preston PR5 0SH
01254 852986
Held on the third Sunday of every month (except July, which is one week earlier than usual).

Hart Brewery

THERE ARE SOME ODD STORIES concerning the beginnings of several micro breweries, but they don't come any stranger than the tale of the Hart Brewery. Back in 1993, the local Preston paper had some fun with a Customs and Excise report. 'Chateau Preston' headlined the case of John Smith, who was caught making his own champagne in his garage. There was also the matter of 350 gallons of beer he had fermenting as well and John was fined an eye-watering sum.

The customs officer who nabbed him happened to be a regular at the Cartford Inn, an utterly delightful country pub by the River Wyre at Little Eccleston – and the landlord at the Cartford, Andrew Mellowdew, happened to be looking for someone to brew beer for the pub. Andrew reckons that great brewers, like goalkeepers and star chefs, have to be ever so slightly dotty. Together they conspired in 1995 to set up John Smith with an entirely legitimate ten-barrel brewery in the disused stable block at the back of the pub. Everyone has lived happily ever after.

The Hart Brewery has produced an impressive array of beers over the years, but Valediction, a delicious black beer with a thick creamy head, is one of the current favourites at the Cartford and elsewhere. Described by John as a typical old English ale, it has collected several prizes, including Beer of the Festival at

Southport's Sandgrounder Festival 2003. Another beer which has caused quite a stir is Deepdale Hooker, a session bitter which pays tribute to both Preston's rugby players and ladies of the night. There's a t-shirt in extremely dubious taste to celebrate the beer. Hart's beers are available in about a hundred outlets, mostly in the North West. There are always one or two on tap at the pub, of course.

 Hart Brewery Co Ltd, Cartford Hotel
Cartford Lane, Little Eccleston, Preston PR3 0YP
01995 671686

Thyme at the Sirloin Inn

AT HOGHTON TOWER, KING JAMES I knighted a loin of beef, 'Arise, Sir Loin!' so, no prizes for guessing that a fine piece of beefsteak is still one of the most popular dishes at this popular, prize-winning gastropub.

Thyme (ahem) does not stand still, however, and above the open-fires, settles and polished horse brasses of the traditional 300-year-old pub, the airy burgundy and clotted cream first-floor restaurant offers a winning formula: good modern food in a contemporary but easygoing setting with an emphasis on local ingredients. Owned by Wayne Keough and Alex Coward, it is one of four popular eating places, including the Sirloin Inn, as well as the Thyme Restaurant and Café and The Forest Arms, both at Longridge.

Sautéed chicken livers with smoked bacon, garlic, marjoram and a splash of cream with homemade toasted brioche is a popular first course. 'Thyme for

Thyme

Specials' might include braised Bowland lamb shoulder with a timbale of haggis, spinach, mashed potatoes and creamed whisky sauce, while those sought-after sirloins come pan-seared with Diane sauce or pot-roasted with a mousse of pancetta and (yes!) thyme, galette potato and red wine jus. Finally, when it's 'Thyme for Indulgence' (well, there's always time for that), try iced prune and aromatic parfait with liquorice ice cream and honey tuile.

The carte changes on a seasonal basis, and much produce is sourced locally, including wines from Ribblesdale Wines in Clitheroe. As well as a wine of the month, there are some exciting exclusives, plus good port to match regional cheeses.

So, don't know how to choose between the beetroot marinated fillet of salmon with sautéed spring cabbage and white wine and chive sauce, and the Thai spiced risotto cakes with baked soy glazed oyster mushrooms, red chard leaves and chilli pesto dressing? Never mind: there's always next thyme.

i **Thyme at the Sirloin Inn**
Station Road, Hoghton, Preston PR5 0DD
012548 52293 www.thyme-restaurant.co.uk

Longridge

Paul Heathcote
Longridge Restaurant

AFTER A CAREER THAT SAW HIM COOKING from the high cuisine kitchens to being the first lieutenant for Raymond Blanc at Le Manoir aux Quat' Saisons, Paul Heathcote returned to his native Lancashire in 1989 to open a fine dining restaurant in the Bleasdale Fells village of Longridge. Warned that his ambition would only end in tears, Paul stuck with his belief that if the food was good, then customers would find the restaurant no matter how far off the main road.

That proved correct and within a couple of years of opening the critics and guide books were full of praise for the mix of classical techniques with North West flavours and recipes. The high point for the Longridge restaurant was when the *Michelin Guide* awarded him two stars for his cooking.

Determined to make good food accessible to every budget, in 1995 Paul launched the Simply Heathcotes and Olive Press concepts. This was to be food of the highest standard, but served in informal surroundings. Simply Heathcotes restaurants are spreading in the North of England, but at a steady pace that allows Paul to ensure each new restaurant meets the high standards he first set in Longridge. Paul has chosen the following dish using local produce.

i **The Longridge Restaurant**
104-106 Higher Road, Longridge, Preston PR3 3SY
01772 784969 www.simplyheathcotes.com

Corn fed chicken with wild mushrooms, leeks and Lancashire goat cheese fritter.

Lancashire Recipe Corn fed Chicken with Wild Mushrooms, Leeks and Lancashire Goat Cheese Fritter

Serves 4

What you need

4 breasts of corn-fed chicken
150g butter
2tbsp finely chopped shallot
Dash of white wine
100ml water
50ml whipping cream
100g of wild mushrooms
8 baby leeks, cooked
4tsp fresh tarragon, finely shredded
Squeeze of lemon juice

What you do

In a thick bottomed pan take 50g of the butter and seal the chicken breast, skin side down.

Add the shallots and white wine.

Bring to the boil, add water, cover with a lid and place in the oven at 180°C until cooked. This should take 10-15 minutes, but check the chicken by pushing a skewer or fork into the middle and looking at the colour of the juice that comes out. If it's clear it's cooked. Remove the chicken and keep it warm.

Strain the liquid through a fine sieve into another pan. Bring to the boil and add the mushrooms and cook for about one minute before adding the cream and boiling until it reduces by half.

Whisk in the butter little by little, add the cooked leeks, chicken and tarragon and serve with the goat cheese fritter.

Season with salt and a good squeeze of lemon, but no pepper.

Lancashire Goat Cheese Fritter

What you need

125g diced butter
150g sifted flour
4 eggs
300ml cold water
175g Gruyère cheese
100g Lancashire goat cheese
Salt and pepper

What you do

Bring the water and butter to the boil and beat in the flour with a wooden spoon till the mixture leaves the side of the pan. Remove from heat.

Place mixture in a food processor and beat until it cools slightly. Gradually add the eggs one at a time. Add the cheese and season to taste.

Deep fry in hot oil till golden on the outside and runny in the centre.

CHEF'S TIPS

- Corn-fed chicken is a lovely sunny yellow colour and is packed with flavour, unlike factory-farmed chicken. In the restaurant I use corn-fed chicken raised by a farmer close by, but supplies are very limited. You can buy locally-produced corn-fed chicken at farmers' markets, or a good local butchers.

- Many cheesemakers in the North West produce some wonderful cheeses. Goat cheese has a sharper flavour than mild cow milk cheese, but putting the Gruyère in adds a little sweetness.

- You must use whipping cream in this recipe to prevent the cream splitting and spoiling the sauce.

- Once you have tasted these cheese fritters you will think of many other ways of using them.

GREATER MANCHESTER

Greater Manchester must be hungry. You can fit in a month of munching on distinct national cuisines from Armenia to Zimbabwe across this great urban sprawl.

GREATER MANCHESTER

PROPER AROMATHERAPY. Plant yourself outside the Barbakan deli in Chorlton-cum-Hardy, Manchester, early in the morning and inhale. You can't miss it, the perfume of baking bread in 30-plus varieties, many destined for the region's top restaurants and retailers. Across the road from Barbakan is the Unicorn Grocery, arguably the country's largest organic and vegetarian co-operative retailer providing the best in regionally grown fruit and veg.

A couple of hundred metres south is the decades-old Frost's butchers which supplies quality cuts for lucky locals, as well as top city restaurants such as Le Mont at Urbis. When the shopping gets too much, the best way to relax is at one of the two Marble Beers outlets here, with their selection of own brand micro brewery ales.

Suburban Chorlton is Greater Manchester food and drink in a nutshell. Cosmopolitan – Barbakan is a Polish deli in origin – progressive and mercurial. It's also a model for a return to the independent, neighbourhood shopping of the past with the added twenty-first century ingredient of higher quality.

Chorlton might be a model, but across Greater Manchester, whether in retail or in restaurants, we're talking excellence. North to south from the maverick genius of Paul Kitching's Juniper restaurant in Altrincham, to Bolton's fish market, through the city centre's eclectic scrum of bars, pubs, shops and restaurants, and via Chinatown and the so-called 'Curry Mile' at Rusholme, there are a thousand exciting food experiences to be found.

Range is the keynote characteristic. Greater Manchester must be hungry. You can fit in a month of munching on distinct national cuisines from Armenia to Zimbabwe across this great urban sprawl. This is especially the case in the central area. Manchester has been at the forefront of making our regional capitals easy places in which to enjoy good food and drink and it's still ahead of the game.

There is nowhere in these islands, with the exception of London, where you can enjoy such variety. For instance, in the half mile from the celebrated Chinese restaurant, Yang Sing, to 2004's gastropub phenomenon The Bridge, you can enjoy one of the most popular independent pizzerias anywhere, Croma (which recently opened a franchise in Boston, Mass), the pricelessly decadent and rude Lounge Ten, or celeb-haunt, Restaurant Bar and Grill.

Of course, given its almost solidly urban character, Greater Manchester is more of a consumer and retailer than a producer of foods and has been for the last hundred years or more. Yet large or small, there's still a great deal of food and drink created in the conurbation. Big boys include multinationals and nationals such as Kelloggs, Heinz, United Biscuits, Brooke Bond, Warburtons and Vimto. Smaller producers include the Barbakan described above, Ho's Bakery in Chinatown, the Little Pickle Company in Oldham, the Saddleworth Sausage Company and real babies such as Osa Spices in Bury, Roma deli ice creams in Prestwich and Dunham Ices close to Dunham Massey Park.

A real strength is brewing. Not only does Greater Manchester boast the largest number of major family brewers in the country – Holts, Hydes, Lees and Robinsons – but also a largish clutch of micros. Incidentally, if you like a splash or two of grog, then the conurbation boasts some superb and quirky drinks retailers such as TH Wrights of Horwich, Carringtons in Chorlton and elsewhere, Winos in Oldham and Portland Wine in Hale.

The Greater Manchester food and drink story is about pedigree too. Most people have heard of Eccles cakes and Manchester tarts but how many know that two eastern districts of the conurbation, Oldham and Mossley, slog it out for the accolade of the first UK fish and chip shop. Mossley has perhaps the stronger challenge with John Lees' purpose-built wooden hut in 1863, set up as an off-shoot of his pig trotter and pea soup operation.

Meanwhile, a true heroine of culinary excellence is the indomitable Elizabeth Raffald. In 1769, this Manchester landlady published perhaps the first commercially successful English cookbook. It was called *The Experienced English Housekeeper* and ran to 13 editions and was pirated at least 23 times. Recipes include: 'To make a Porcupine breast of veal' and 'To make moon and stars in jelly'. In 1773 she sold the copyright for £1,400.

Nor is it any accident that the National Vegetarian Society is based in Altrincham. This owes its origin to an 1809 sermon by a Salford preacher, called of all things, the Reverend William Cowherd. A vegetarian cookbook by local woman Martha Brotherton followed in 1812.

Past or present, Greater Manchester is a place to enjoy food and drink, a place to celebrate it, revel in it. To paraphrase Woody Allen, food and drink is the best fun you can have with your clothes on. These were the delights of a home-cooked childhood in Greater Manchester: full breakfasts with local black pudding and farm eggs, homemade bread and soups, cow-heel pies, hotpots, tripe with lashings of vinegar, stews, dumplings, fish, trifles, cakes, apple tarts, rhubarb tarts, gooseberry tarts, ginger biscuits, oaties, homemade raspberry jam. The list goes on and on.

Good food never really went away, it merely faded into the background for a while. We must thank the food gods, farmers, retailers and customers, for this return to a less homogenised world. During one of the farmers' markets in Albert Square, Manchester, last Christmas, a young person with a strong Mancunian accent declared loudly, 'I always get bacon in the farmers' markets, if I pass one. It's got taste, real taste.' Well, exactly.

Love Saves the Day

LOVE SAVES THE DAY (LStD) is a model for all funky, urban food and drink venues. This is an all-in-one coffee shop, deli and bistro housed in a splendid former department store. To enjoy quality food and drink amidst warm woods and handsome cast iron pillars is a real Mancunian pleasure.

Amy Cook

Drinks-wise, alongside the usual range of coffee choices, cappuccinos and lattes, there's the in-house Northern Quarter coffee blend, and around ten herbal and traditional teas. Other drinks include wines and beers, which are available from the wine department for only £4 corkage, as well as smoothies and so on. The enterprising menu, with its daily specials, covers the ground between soups and sweets via substantial mains with typical LStD panache. The smart selection of wines is notable especially for those of Italian provenance. There's an enterprising events programme too.

One of the best pastimes in LStD is people watching. The Northern Quarter of Manchester is the beating heart of Manchester's creative industries. You might be nibbling the latest cheesy lovely from Raven's Oak Dairy whilst sitting next to a prominent DJ, or the singer from the next big thing.

Beckie Joyce, co-proprietor of Love Saves the Day, is pleased about how things have turned out. May 2004 was the fifth birthday of the business and she now feels that her business is very much part of Manchester. One of her initiatives has been to bolster the stock sourced from regional food producers. The main local items they stock are chutneys, cheese, hams and so on. LStD customers are very opinionated, very in touch with current issues and they appreciate being given the choice of buying locally.

Joyce still feels that one crucial element of support for regional food and drink is still lacking. It's time for central government to take regional food and drink promotion to the next level, to support these industries from the very top as cultural assets as they do in France. Given the popularity and quality of food and drink in this busy and buzzy city centre establishment, it would seem that many other UK citizens feel the same.

i **Love Saves the Day**
Oldham Street, Manchester M4 1LE
0161 832 0777

Love Saves the Day
345 Deansgate, Manchester M3 4LG
0161 834 2266

www.lovesavestheday.com

Slattery

Amy Cook

ASKED WHETHER FAMILIARITY MIGHT BREED CONTEMPT for his most popular product, John Slattery explodes with laughter declaring that, on the contrary, he's a chocolate addict and eats it every day.

Slattery is the north Manchester King of Confection, the Prince of Patisserie. A visit to his shop and dining rooms is a lesson in indulgence with more than 40 varieties of exquisitely sculpted chocolate, plus gateaux, desserts and puddings. Once sated on these, visitors are often inspired to take advantage of the bespoke service in larger cakes. Slattery will sculpt anything you want from novelties such as 'Top Table', a wedding scene with a tipsy mother-in-law, to in-house classics such as the glorious Orangina. The dining room which royally repays dalliance, offers excellent snacks and meals, sturdy coffees, fine wines and, of course, all manner of cakes and pastries.

The popularity has been such that John found he had to publish his own book, *Chocolate Cakes for Weddings and Celebrations*, which has sold 15,000 copies. Another highly valued off-shoot is the Slattery School of Excellence for those, amateur and professional, who wish unravel the mysteries of the chocolatier.

The key to the business is consistency, a reputation of excellence and value for money. Above all, Slattery and his staff try to adhere to the philosophy that the customer comes first. Clearly these old fashioned qualities have worked and the number of staff in the 37-year-old company has risen to 35.

In early 2004 he moved across the road to the former Mason's Arms. This was to give customers and staff more room to move but also to allow the further development of the school and conferencing facilities. There's an added feature too, surely a first for Whitefield – a roof terrace. This is stirring up a lot of interest. Not that everybody is familiar with local geography. One lady asked if she'd be able to see the sea. Not quite. The Pennines maybe, although most will find it difficult to see beyond their profiterole pyramids or Charlotte rousses.

i **Slattery, Patissier and Chocolatier**
197 Bury New Road, Whitefield, Manchester M45 6GE
0161 767 9303 www.slattery.co.uk

Uncle Joe's Mint Balls

William Santus & Co Ltd

TO THIS DAY THE PROCESS of producing Wigan's most famous confectionery remains a closely guarded secret, known only to the current managing directors. What is certain, however, about Uncle Joe's Mint Balls, is that they are free from additives and artificial colours – completely natural, GM free and suitable for vegans and vegetarians. Perhaps even more remarkably they still follow the original recipe devised in 1898 by Mrs Santus, wife of William Santus, founder of the company that still produces Uncle Joe's Mint Balls.

The eponymous Uncle Joe with his beatific smile and dandyish top hat, whose face appears on every tin of mint balls, has inspired an affectionate reaction in the public imagination over the years. There have been cartoons, songs and poems dedicated to the figurehead of the William Santus Company and to his much cherished mints. One of the old music hall songs includes the following memorable lines:

Uncle Joe's mint balls keep you all aglow
Give them to your granny and watch the beggar go.

Whatever lies behind the mystery, the recipe for the mint balls packs a powerful global punch drawing plaudits from as far afield as India, Kenya and America. Of course, nostalgia plays a huge part in the appeal of Uncle Joe's. Tradition is woven through the fabric of the company like the heat in the sweets. This is especially apparent in Uncle Joe's Emporium in Crompton Street, Wigan. Here you can partake of a selection of sweets from 140 large jars including Mint Balls, Pear Drops, Humbugs, Sarsaparilla Drops, Menthol and Eucalyptus and Pontefract Cakes.

Uncle Joe is the closest to a real Willy Wonka that Britain has ever produced. Long may his sweets light fires in the belly of the world.

 William Santus & Co Ltd
The Toffee Works, Dorning Street, Wigan WN1 1HE
01942 243464 www.uncle-joes.com

Vimto

THE FOUNDING FATHER OF VIMTO, John Noel Nichols was a bit of a chancer. At the beginning of the twentieth century he was looking for a way into the lucrative market for health tonics and temperance drinks. In 1908, in his Frankenstein-style lab on Granby Row in central Manchester he hit upon a particular mix of herbs, spices, roots and essences. It was a winner. He called his new cordial Vimto from the first word of the well-known expression 'vim and vigour' and the first letters of tonic.

J N Nichols (Vimto) Ltd has now moved out of the city west to Newton-le-

Willows. It remains one of the major food and drinks companies in the North West with a variety of interests, but it's still the herbal drink, which is the core of the business. If you want some fun then check out the entertaining website. This comes complete with stunning facts such as 458 Vimto bottles stacked upright would be equivalent in height to Blackpool Tower.

Manchester's contribution to the soft drinks hall of fame is splendidly commemorated on the site of 49 Granby Row in the city centre in the gardens adjacent to UMIST. Here sculptor Kerry Morrison has placed a three-metre high timber Vimto bottle on the site where the drink was first concocted. It took five months to create but Morrison was relieved to find that she was provided with all the Vimto she could drink. In other words she needed all the vim and vigour she could get.

i **Vimto Ltd, Laurel House**
Woodlands Park, Ashton Road, Newton-le-Willow WA12 0HH
01925 222222 www.vimto.co.uk

Urbis

Amy Cook

EARLY IN 2004 THERE WERE 30 CHIEF EXECUTIVES from regional French airports in Le Mont six floors up in Manchester city centre. They were exploring how links between Liverpool and Manchester airports could be developed. It was their first night and the dramatic location in an exciting new building, together with executive chef Robert Kisby's food, was working wonders. The clever assiette was the star for the tastebuds, putting a Gallic accent on dishes such as Lancashire hotpot and kidney and mushroom pie. Monsieur Arles Airport was struggling with some vernacular English to express the moment, finally he smiled, sighed and just nodded.

But it would be a strange person who was unmoved by the first sight of Urbis, a visitor attraction devoted to the study of urban cultures. Manchester practice, Ian Simpson Architects, have produced a building, which inside and out is a jaw-dropper: a harmonious sweep of glass, steel, concrete and copper etched into the city skyline. It's only been up since 2002 and it's impossible to imagine the city without it. Buildings such as Urbis, and the Imperial War Museum North three miles west, add to the prestige of a city region.

This means a fatter slice of the tourist cake, locally, nationally and internationally. It's even better for the new icons of a city if they are supported by catering as good as that provided by Le Mont on Levels 5/6 and its sister operation, the Conservatory on the ground floor.

Chef Robert Kisby knows his responsibilities too. As long as he can get good consistency with supply and best quality in the end-product, then he sources a large portion of his ingredients regionally. As he acknowledges, ten years ago this wouldn't have been possible. He gives a lot of credit to the growth in quantity and reliability of supply to fellow chefs Paul Heathcote and Nigel Haworth in Lancashire. It was these two, in particular, who first began to ask some North West farmers to change their mindset and become more individual and specialised. Kisby gets lamb from Bowland, Lune Valley venison, fish from the Fylde coast and so on. He uses Manchester butcher, Frost's, for cuts of meat too and there are always a couple of regional cheeses. One advantage of this, for Kisby, is that it shows care, authenticity and boosts the business's credibility. Diners respect regional sourcing, simple as that.

i **Urbis**
Cathedral Gardens, Manchester M4 3BG
0161605 8200 www.urbis.org.uk

Unicorn Grocery

THE SURVIVAL AND EXPANSION OF THIS GROCERY, a workers' co-operative in 2003, was remarkable. Threatened by the redevelopment of their building, Unicorn needed money and quickly. They started a loan stock scheme where people could invest in the shop and get their investment back in five years. Within a week £100,000 had been pledged, enough to put an offer into the landlord. Before a month was out £300,000 had been raised from the loan stock, and more came in from commercial mortgages and loans from various ethical companies to secure the property outright. Has there ever been a more impressive example of customer loyalty in the North West?

Now the shop boasts extra shop floor space and better access all round. The

119

Amy Cook

food counter stocks fresh wholesome snacks and delicacies such as salads, marinated olives, cakes and pastries. There is an excellent organic range of whole foods, beers and cider. The selection of organic wines is the best in the North by a country mile, whilst the wide range of fruit and veg section uses many local lines and is a magnet for those looking for real flavour – very fairly priced.

Elsewhere, customers can pick up environmentally and ethically screened goods, household cleaners and toiletries. Items can be picked up as bulk purchases to reduce excess packaging and cost. Local suppliers are used where possible, whilst GM free and high quality standards are present throughout. There is even a good play area for kids and a great organic baby food and baby care range. Turnover currently stands at around £1.5 million and if the weekend queues are anything to judge by, then that figure is due to grow further. The notice boards offer good advice on food issues and even post relevant newspaper articles.

i **Unicorn Grocery**
89 Albany Road, Chorlton, Manchester M21 0BM
www.unicorn-grocery.co.uk

Barbakan

Amy Cook

THE BARBAKAN IS NOT JUST A LEGEND IN THE SOUTH MANCHESTER area but far beyond too. A legend for its 40-plus types of bread including Polish black, Norlander rye, Margarita olive, brown caraway seed, cheese and sun dried tomato, plus baguettes, pretzels and cakes and pastries. And also for the range of traditional deli foods of principally Italian, German and Polish origin, complemented by locally-sourced produce. In the last few years the already high reputation has been reinforced by a splendid assortment of prepared dishes, salads, sandwiches, teas, coffees and juices.

The breads in particular illustrate why the Barbakan is so popular, carrying the robust flavours and rich textures that seem the domain of small-scale, independent producers. Eating a Barbakan loaf feels good for you in a way that anodyne supermarket bread fails to do. Not that it's a serious business. Sample a rosemary and roast potato loaf and – love it or loathe it – you'll be impressed.

The Barbakan story began in 1964 when a Mr Zaremba, from the Krakow region in Poland, decided to open a bakery in Chorlton. The name was borrowed from the main marketplace in Krakow. Zaremba's aim was to serve the large local community of Polish emigrés. Presently the business is owned by Stefan and Joanna Najduch, who acquired it in 1986. Their vision was to turn it into a more conventional deli. This, with a few tweaks, is what we see today,.

except now it is a much bigger operation. With a staff of 43 and a team of 13 full-time bakers who turn out between 8,000 and 10,000 loaves per week, they supply many of the city's top restaurants, Selfridges and Harvey Nicholls food halls, as well as the shop customers.

Four decades of survival as an independent food retailer is impressive by any measure. Either someone buys you out, fashions change, or something bigger opens nearby that blows you out of the water. The Barbakan has resisted all that and expanded into the bargain, which is quite an achievement.

Barbakan Delicatessen Ltd
67-70 Manchester Road, Chorlton-cum-Hardy,
Manchester M21 9PW
0161 881 7053

Redhouse Farm Shop and Tearoom

Redhouse Tearoom

IN SUMMER IT'S EASY TO GET LOST AT REDHOUSE FARM. But at least they give you a flag to wave to attract the attention of the rescue party. This is the way farms have to think in the early twenty-first century. It's not so much diversifying as multi-tasking.

Redhouse Farm started selling eggs and potatoes direct to the public 30 years ago, now, aside from the maize maze alluded to above, there is a flourishing farm shop and tearoom that have become a very pleasurable part of life for many south Manchester people. Jonathan Hewitt of Redhouse Farm sees this as part of a process in rural areas of the UK and puts forward the controversial thesis that crises such as Foot and Mouth were amongst the best things that could have happened to UK agriculture. It was horrible at the time, of course, but it made many people think about what they were doing and how they approached farm operation.

At the same time as Foot and Mouth, people were becoming bored with supermarkets and wanted something a little more individual. Many farmers realised this was a market that could be exploited. The food in the Redhouse farm shop illustrates this.

Customers appreciate locally-sourced produce as long as it's of good quality. The manic weekend of trade in early May 2004 at the start of Cheshire new potatoes clearly underlined this point. Redhouse is trying to develop the local foodstuffs all the time. To complement the good quality fruit and veg, they have local cheeses, meats, jams and chutneys. A real favourite is the Cartmel Sticky Toffee Pudding. Crucially, the farm shop is developing a broad client base of regular shoppers as well as tourists. So what's next in the Redhouse expansion programme? Hewitt, it turns out, has been on reconnoitring tours of the States. Expect something spectacular at Halloween.

i **Redhouse Farm Shop and Tearoom**
Redhouse Lane, Dunham Massey, Altrincham WA14 5RL
0161 941 3480 www.redhousefarm.co.uk

Ashton under Lyne Farmers' Market

WHAT IAN KELLY, ASHTON MARKET'S business development manager, loves about the farmers' market is the broad section of the community who enjoy the event. Despite some reports to the contrary, regional and speciality foods are not the sole preserve of the green welly brigade looking for fashionable foods. The Ashton mix of people creates a real buzz to the market. There's a lot of laughter and talk but also a great deal of learning, with people asking the suppliers about the different products.

It's not just chat either. Suppliers find that their visits to Ashton make financial sense as long as they learn some essential lessons. Some of the farmers found the events hard going at first. They had to develop skills in customer service that they'd not previously needed. Once they had these they found that people are happy to pay a premium for a personal guarantee of

The Bluecoat Press

quality. This makes sense: the connection here between customer and producer is very close and that matters. The public also realise that with lower commercial volumes the price rises a little but variety increases. People love the fact that Ashton, for instance, has varieties of potato not seen for 100 years, such as the rich and buttery Pink Fir Apple potatoes from Cheshire.

Ashton farmers' market takes place on the last Sunday of every month. There is a large range of food available, examples being, venison, vegetables, cheese, honey, chutney, lamb, smoked fish, ostrich, home bake, fudge and so on. The basic rule is that produce should be from within a 50-mile radius of Ashton. Of course, there's a degree of flexibility, thus Greek olives are allowed, which although not grown locally, are bottled nearby. To add to the sense of occasion, events are organised around the market. Popular ones have included Asian and Spanish chefs using local ingredients during cooking demonstrations.

So what's Ian Kelly's favourite supplier on the market? The market's man confesses to a certain partiality for the honeycomb ice creams that the ladies from Dunham Massey Farm bring along. Who can blame him? The flesh is weak after all.

Ashton Farmers' Market
Bow Street, Ashton under Lyne
0161 342 3268
The market takes place on the last Sunday of every month.

Phoenix Brewery

LOOK CAREFULLY AROUND HEYWOOD'S PUBS and you will find one or two reminders of the original Phoenix Brewery – a stained glass window here, a tessellated entrance hall there. The brewery, which had been founded in the mid-nineteenth century, was closed by Bass in the 1960s, and the premises taken over by a myriad of small businesses.

One of the incomers in 1991 was Tony Allen's Oak Brewery, from Ellesmere Port. Tony, a pioneer of micro breweries in this part of the world, had started up on an industrial estate on Merseyside, but the business was successful and had outgrown the site. Eventually he decided that the old brewery name might be a strong marketing ploy. In 1996, the Oak became Phoenix, although it still only occupied a corner of the huge original palatial red brick building.

Phoenix is arguably the best known and most successful of the region's micros, supplying over four hundred outlets nationwide. Tony has produced literally hundreds of different beers over the years. The current *Good Beer Guide* lists over 30 in current seasonal production. Some have become well known nationally and are still produced on a regular basis. Wobbly Bob, a

The Bluecoat Press

dangerously strong reddish beer, named after a cat that fell over when it turned corners, has won Silver (1998) and Gold (2002) medals at the International Brewing Awards, a prestigious competition held each year in Burton on Trent. Navvy, a session bitter, won a Gold in its category here as well in 2002. Monkeytown Mild, a dark luscious brew, commemorates a scurrilous old folk tale that Heywood folk had tails. Arizona, a straw coloured beer made with American hops, is popular in scores of the region's pubs.

i   **Phoenix Brewery**
Green Lane, Heywood OL10 2EP
01706 627009

The Bridge

THE BRIDGE HAS BEEN A BIG HIT AND THEN SOME. Proprietor chef Robert Owen Brown, hard-worked in a kitchen slightly smaller than an ice cream van, finds the exposure a pleasure. As he himself understands, whilst not being a case of too much too soon, it's meant that he's had to work hard to satisfy large numbers of guests at a time when this new gastropub was bedding in.

Still he's a big man, with broad shoulders, who tells it as it is. He'll chop and he'll cut through some of the nonsense in cooking whilst he's about it. Jay Rayner of the *Observer* once asked him on a visit why he called the peas on the menu peas and not petit pois. Owen Brown pointed out that the peas weren't French, the food wasn't French and he wasn't French, so why should he put them in French? Especially as, he might have added, the Bridge was built during the Napoleonic Wars.

Owen Brown's cooking is on the surface as direct as the man. But what makes his work special is an extra ingredient of sophistication. Take a main dish like poached fillet of plaice with sweet baby vegetables and a shellfish broth. It's sort of perfect: rich fishy creamed-up stock, with prawns and mussels, courgettes, chives and spring onions tumbling about. The plaice, a fish that's easy to cook in a dull way, is here a delicate glory balanced on a soft but sturdy mash potato.

Even the presentation is exemplary – whites, pinks, oranges and greens artfully arranged. The prices are a bargain too.

The pub itself plays an active role in any visit. Smartly painted in red with handsome wooden fittings, it dates back to 1794 and feels it, especially in the

The Bridge

marvellous dining and function room upstairs. This latter was once the home of the Manchester Glee Club but by the mid-nineteenth century, the pub found itself part of the hard-drinking District 13, which attracted notoriety for the number of its brothels – 46 in less than half a square kilometre. Later the pub would have to survive developers, the Blitz, bad landlords and a spell as a topless bar.

Yet durability is part of the genius of the British boozer. Despite taking the knocks, places like the Bridge carry on, picking up personality as they go. The old pub has found an equally durable companion in Robert Owen Brown who has previously run the kitchens in Manchester landmarks such as The Reform, Lounge Ten, and Sam's Chop House. The Bridge is his magnificent stride into independence. The city has got lucky.

  The Bridge
58 Bridge Street, Manchester M3 3BW
0161 834 0242

Amy Cook

Robert Kisby
Le Mont

ROBERT KISBY HAS HAD TWO PASSIONS IN HIS CAREER – good cooking and encouraging young chefs to come into the restaurant kitchen. One of his early inspirational chefs was the legendary Gilbert Lefevre, who established the then-named Manchester Midland Hotel as one of the swishest dining destinations in the city, with a team of 50 chefs, the largest kitchen team in the city.

After working at other North West restaurants, Robert went back to the Midland Hotel in 1989, as senior sous chef for eight years. In the mid-1990s Robert was asked to turn the newly developed Bridgewater Hall into a food destination and his success there led him to his current position of company executive chef. He cooks in one of Manchester's most talked about dining establishments, Le Mont, the restaurant at the Urbis Centre. The food has a Gallic leaning, but running through the menu is evidence that Robert believes a good local restaurant should have North West flavours and ingredients. Nowhere is this more evident on the Le Mont menu than with this restaurant's favourite using lamb from the Forest of Bowland.

 Le Mont Restaurant
Urbis, Cathedral Gardens, Manchester M4 3BG
0161 605 8282 www.urbis.co.uk

Assiette of Bowland lamb with red wine rosemary sauce.

Assiette of Bowland Lamb with Red Wine Rosemary Sauce

Serves 4

What you need

4 x 140g racks of local lamb (this should be two connected cutlets)
2 lamb kidneys
50g lamb liver, cut into four slices
100g lamb shoulder cut into a very fine dice
50g mushrooms, finely sliced
2 medium onions
2 carrots
1 stick of celery
1 small swede
4 green Savoy cabbage leaves
1 large potato and one medium onion (for Boulangère potatoes)
100g shortcrust pastry
1tsp parsley
1.5 litres chicken stock
25g shallots, finely chopped
100ml Madeira
100ml red wine
Sprig of rosemary, finely chopped

What you do

Wash, prepare and cut into 1/2cm dice the onion, carrot, swede and celery.

In a hot pan, lightly oiled, seal the diced shoulder of lamb, add the vegetables, enough chicken stock to cover and cook slowly as for hotpot.

Line four mini brioche moulds with shortcrust pastry, rest for 30 minutes and bake blind.

Blanch the cabbage leaves in boiling water for about 45 seconds until they wilt, then cool in iced water.

Line four ramekin moulds with the blanched cabbage, buttering and seasoning the moulds first. Fill cabbage parcels with hotpot stew reserving excess cooking liquor to make red wine sauce. Fold over the cabbage leaf to make the cabbage parcel.

Prepare the Boulangère potatoes by finely slicing the onion and potato. Sweat the onion gently in a little oil or butter until soft, but not brown. Layer onion and potato seasoning as you build the layers. Potato is the top layer. Add some chicken stock and bake in the oven until the potato is soft and crisp brown on top.

Taking a hot frying pan, seal off the four lamb racks, season and place in oven to roast to the preferred degree of cooking. I like my lamb pink. Remove and rest for ten minutes.

In a small pan, sweat off finely the chopped shallots, then add finely sliced mushrooms and diced kidneys.

Deglaze the pan with the Madeira, add the chopped parsley, bind with a little cooking liquor and set aside.

Using any vegetable trimmings left after peeling and chopping, sweat them in a little oil or butter, deglaze the pan with the red wine, reduce to a syrupy consistency and add the leftover hotpot cooking liquid and continue to reduce to a sauce consistency. When reduced, pass through a fine sieve, season with salt and pepper to taste and set aside.

Amy Cook

To present the dish

Reheat cabbage hotpot parcels and Boulangère potatoes.

Fill pastry tartlets with the kidney mix.

Turn cabbage hotpot parcels on to plate.

Cut racks of lamb in half and cut out the eye of one of the chops. Place the whole cutlet on top of the hotpot and eye on top of the Boulangère potatoes.

Flour the slices of liver and pan fry. Thinly slice the livers and fan out on top of the kidney tartlet.

Finish the red wine sauce with chopped rosemary and pour around the plate.

CHEF'S TIPS

- Assiette is a French word meaning plate. This dish is a selection of cuts and presentations of lamb on one plate.

- A good local butcher will be able to select and prepare the lamb racks for you and ask him to trim any excess fat.

- Much of this recipe can be prepared in advance and re-heated prior to serving without any loss of flavour. It also ensures everything is hot when it reaches the table.

MERSEYSIDE

Photo The Bluecoat Press

This mercantile, cosmopolitan heritage has endowed Merseyside with a rich culinary identity which manifests itself in modern-day businesses.

MERSEYSIDE

THINK OF MERSEYSIDE AS AN IMAGINARY GIANT OCTOPUS, with tentacles wrapping around the four corners of the earth and you'll understand how its culinary diversity evolved.

Along each of these arms once plied regular shipping lines, each adding to the melting pot character of the great northern seaport. Blue Funnel to the Far East and Australasia (whose cooks established Europe's oldest Chinese community); Blue Star Line (part of Liverpool's Vestey family meat empire) to Argentina; Booth Line to Spain, Madeira and Brazil; Pacific Steam Navigation to Central America, Peru and Chile; Elder Dempster's to East Africa and Fyffes to the Caribbean (both lines introduced bananas to Britain via Liverpool); Anchor Line and Harrison Line to India; Cunard and Canadian Pacific to North America.

Aboard these sturdy ships came the exotic spices, teas and coffees of the import trade; also came the traditional foods brought by the Chinese, Irish, Indian, Jewish, Swedish, Chilean and German crews and passengers. Some of these souls were transient, while others created their own communities. Of Russian-Polish descent the Liverpool-born writer Linda Grant recalls how her father worked pre-war aboard Cunard Line's RMS *Laconia* as a 'Jew baker' in the ship's kosher galley. Many British got their first taste of American fast food aboard Cunard and CP liners which, besides haute cuisine, served them alien dishes like cheese burgers, clam chowder, grits and even Seven Up in their soda bars.

Most famously, the Norwegians bequeathed Liverpool its signature dish scouse, a name applied to Liverpudlians themselves. The port's warehouses were piled high with spices, coffee beans and tea-exotica which we now take for granted.

Big hotels like the North Western and Adelphi catered for transatlantic traffic that ranged from presidents to immigrants, gentlemen's clubs like the Athenaeum and Lyceum served the merchant prince élite. From the late eighteenth century, Liverpool boasted oyster houses, steak houses and coffee houses (leading to the long-lived Kardomah chain), Harrison Line imported Burgundy and Bordeaux wines via its service to Cahente. These were unloaded at Albert Dock into premises now occupied by the Est Est Est restaurant.

This mercantile, cosmopolitan heritage has endowed Merseyside with a rich culinary identity which manifests itself in modern-day businesses like Seasoned Pioneers, a treasure house of the world's most exotic spices, and in adventurous chefs such as Marc Verité at the Warehouse Brasserie at Southport.

Start your food odyssey at Liverpool's Chinatown, the oldest in the country. As well as the numerous restaurants, such as the Far East, there are several Chinese supermarkets offering the essential ingredients for those who want to experiment with oriental cooking at home. For comforting kosher cuisine, the best thing is to head out to Allerton and Childwall and tuck into a sweet bagel smothered in salty smoked salmon and tangy cream cheese.

Across the Mersey, in leafy Wirral, the warm coastal conditions of the peninsula provide a great climate for cultivating crops. Many farms encourage visitors to pick their own produce during the summer. Claremont Farm, near Bebington, for example, offers its own homegrown asparagus in season as well as all summer soft fruits.

The peninsula has also kept its cattle farmers. Enjoy luxury Brimstage ice cream from Lord Leverhulme's Jersey herds still based at Brimstage, or buy local meat from the butcher Callum Edge, of New Ferry, who works closely with local farmers and is able to offer full traceability. He also specialises in rare breeds, bringing a real traditional taste back to the dinner table.

For quality wines, Scatchards, in Hoylake and Liverpool, can recommend something to go along with your regional produce. For beer lovers there are at least five microbreweries in the county – to find out more visit www.merseycamra.org.uk. Tired travellers can find excellent food and drink at the Baltic Fleet on Wapping near Albert Dock, a pub still steeped in the mercantile history of Liverpool.

Sweet things are also a speciality of the city, a clear reminder of Liverpool's history as a centre of the sugar trade. Today Billingtons is the only importer of unrefined sugar in the country. Everton toffee and mints are well known and widely available today, although sadly the original Everton toffee shop, established in 1753 by Molly Bushell, is no more.

Further up the coast is Formby, where the sandiness of the soil is perfect for growing asparagus. Now the industry is kept alive by people such as David Brooks of Lark Hill Farm, who distributes to restaurants, pubs and shops during this succulent vegetable's short season in May and June.

The perception of Merseyside as an urbanised sprawl does no justice to its true character. Over 35 per cent of the county's total area is agricultural or woodland. The fertile farmland is ideal for growing a wide variety of vegetable and hot house crops, particularly tomatoes. Flavourfresh Salads, at Banks, is still winning awards for its tomatoes and scooped one at the North West Producer of the Year Awards.

Farmers' markets are a great place to discover the best of local produce and across Merseyside their numbers are growing. There's now one twice a month in Liverpool as well as monthly markets in Southport, Bootle, Maghull and Wirral.

For a small county, Merseyside boasts a growing number of niche producers with a real sense of adventure, offering commitment to top quality produce. So whether it's in a village, town or the city, there's always something worth tasting and savouring.

Scouse

FFP

IF ASKED TO NAME A FAMOUS MERSEYSIDE DISH most people would probably pick scouse. It is to Liverpool, what bouillabaisse is to Marseilles, or hotpot is to Lancashire; this meat and vegetable stew, which also lends its name to the local dialect, holds a special place in the hearts of Liverpudlians.

Its origins are fairly obscure, but the theory is that it came from Scandinavia, brought over by sailors when Liverpool was a thriving port in the nineteenth century. From there its popularity as a dish spread and even reached the workhouses, where it was served up to inmates in the mid-1800s. One recipe consisted of 1oz beef, 15oz potato and one gallon of water – all boiled up together.

Arguments rage over which meat and vegetables should be included in the dish but the truth is that scouse was made with whatever was available. Traditionally it's a stew of lamb or beef, vegetables and potatoes.

Like the variations of its ingredients, trying to establish its origins brings up different theories. It seems it was known as 'lobskaus' in Scandinavia, and in Wales, a different version, is still known today as 'lobscouse'. *Duden's*

Etymological Dictionary defines lobskaus as the Low German name of a sailors' stew of meat, fish and potatoes but that the name derives from the English lobscouse, implying that it possibly originated in Liverpool.

The *Oxford English Dictionary* just states that lobscouse is a word of obscure origin, though it does conjecture that 'lob' may be connected with a northern dialect word meaning 'to bubble'. If you speak to older people from the region they will tell you that 'lob' describes the moment when the potatoes have been boiled for too long and they drop in the water; a term which can also apply to vegetables.

So it looks as though its origins will always remain obscure but today, by using the quality beef and lamb from the region – and obviously a different recipe from that of the workhouse – it is a dish to relish, served with lashings of red cabbage and crusty bread.

Bartons Pickles

STEP INTO ANY HOME IN ST HELENS, take a look in the kitchen cupboards and you will probably find a jar of Bartons' legendary pickles.

The people of St Helens are very loyal to Bartons, not just because it is a local company, with its headquarters still in the heart of the town, but because of the high quality and taste of their products.

Business in the Community

Distinctive Product

Most famous is their Piccalilli, which is still made to the original recipe created by Edmund and Lydia Barton. They started by pickling their vegetables in the kitchen and selling them from the back door, nearly 100 years ago. It is still very much a family affair and Joanna Jenner, the great granddaughter of Edmund is now at the helm (photographed, centre, with HRH The Prince of Wales at the BiTC Local Sourcing launch 2003).

Traditionally, the people of St Helens love to have pickles, such as red cabbage, with their hotpots and stews as well as with salads giving them an all-year round popularity.

The Bartons policy is to source ingredients locally where they can and to buy British where possible. Though they no longer need to go knocking on doors to sell their products, they still deliver to homes in the local area and their pickles can also be found in independent shops and local supermarkets.

At present there are 18 pickles, sauces and chutneys in the Bartons range but they are constantly trying new ideas such as Chillilli, a twist on their traditional recipe with a bit more kick. 2005 is the company's centenary and a special range is being planned to celebrate.

i **Bartons Pickles**
Lascelles Street, St Helens WA9 1BA
01744 22593 www.bartonspickles.com

Seasoned Pioneers

SEASONED PIONEERS WAS BORN OF ONE MAN'S DREAM to produce the finest spices, chillies, herbs and exotic blends in the UK. Mark Steene started by slow roasting spices in the small kitchen of his Liverpool flat, trying to recreate the flavours and smells he'd discovered on his backpacking trips around India.

He spent five years perfecting his blends to ensure a true authentic taste and though he has now expanded into factory premises in Liverpool, all the spices are still slow roasted in small batches to ensure quality. His catalogue lists 150 spices and herbs including 50 blends and 50 organic spices drawn from countries as far apart as Indonesia and Mexico.

His efforts have earned the praise of food writers across the country including Nigel Slater, Rick Stein and Nigella Lawson. Mark combs the world for such delicacies as Spanish Pimenton, Middle Eastern Sumac berries and Telicherry peppercorns from the Indian Malabar Coast, so he can make them easily accessible to people in the UK.

Award-winning Producer

Mark makes his own traditional blends. For example, baharat from the Middle East, is an unusual blend of cardamom, allspice and ginger and the fiery African blend of berbere combines, among others, red chillies, fenugreek, cardamom and ajowan.

One of the most popular blends with customers is Ras al Hanout (Arabic for 'top of the shop'), which won the Best Ingredient Award in the 2004 North West Producer of the Year Competition.

Slow roasting allows all the flavours to come together and develop, in contrast to commercial blends where the flavour is just thrown together. Another key factor is the packaging – his spices come in small, resealable foil-wrapped packets, to retain their maximum freshness. All the spices are available through mail order, the internet and can be found at Sainsbury's and at independent retailers across the region.

i **Seasoned Pioneers**
101 Summers Road, Brunswick Business Park,
Liverpool L3 4BJ
0800 0682348 (UK only) or 0151 709 9330
www.seasonedpioneers.co.uk

Drink

Cains Fine Raisin Beer

Robert Cain & Co Ltd

IT'S FAIR TO SAY THAT CAINS BREWERY, which claims 150 years of tradition in Liverpool, has had a chequered existence, since the original Cain family sold out in the 1920s. The latest revival of the company is down to brothers Ajmail and Sudaghara Dusanj, who bought the business in July 2002 and turned it round, with a mixture of charm, determination and extremely hard work.

The new head brewer they brought with them from the Midlands was David Nijs. David has not only kept the original portfolio of beers up to scratch, but has developed a couple of show stoppers of his own – Cains 2008, a bitter, which celebrates Liverpool's successful bid to be the City of Culture in 2008, and the quite extraordinary invention that is Cains Fine Raisin Beer.

The beer first appeared in a bottled version – and promptly won the Tesco Beer Challenge in the autumn of 2003. Under the terms of the win, the bottles were only sold in Tesco stores for an initial period of four months – now they are generally available. There is a draught cask version, which is sold not only in all Cains pubs, but also in around 140 outlets run by the pub company Punch Taverns.

Fine Raisin Beer is strong, at 5 per cent, and is made from optic malt and hopped with styrian goldings – Californian raisins are added at the mash. The result is spice on the nose, booming fruit and effervescence on the palate, with a long finish with more fruit and malt. Beer guru Roger Protz recently selected it as a perfect beer to accompany a dessert including ice cream, at a prestigious dinner organised by the North West branch of the British Beer and Pub Association in Manchester.

There's really no need to wait for a special occasion – Cains Fine Raisin Beer is a wonderful drink whatever the circumstances.

i   **Robert Cain and Co Ltd**
Stanhope Street, Liverpool, Merseyside L8 5XJ
0151 709 8734 www.cains.co.uk

Southport Potted Shrimps

James Peel and NWFF

SMALL, BROWN AND SWEET-TASTING, potted shrimps were once a popular tea-time treat and one producer is making sure this Merseyside-born delicacy remains alive for future generations to enjoy.

Business first really began to boom when the growth of the railways helped to open up the market. As Southport became more accessible, people started to flock to the resort and when they tasted the sweet shrimps they wanted to be able to eat them at home.

Despite the advent of the railways, by the time the shrimps arrived at places such as Wigan or Manchester, they were sometimes unfit to eat. So someone came up with the idea of potted shrimps; by cooking the shelled shrimps, packing them in butter and flavouring them with mace, cayenne and other herbs and spices they would last longer.

James Peet, of Banks, near Southport, is now one of the few producers still selling them. His father went dredging the shores for shrimps when he was young but it became more and more difficult to earn a living from just shrimping without using a boat, so James became an engineer. However, he eventually decided to go back to his roots and started to sell his own secret recipe for potted shrimps through local shops and via mail order.

In the pre-freezer age the shrimps had to be mixed with herbs and spices such as pepper but now the recipe can be lighter. James will admit to using mace and, of course, salt and pepper, but that's all he will reveal.

i **James Peet**
66 Station Road, Banks Village, PR9 8BB
01704 229266 www.pottedshrimp.co.uk

The Everyman and Hope Street

IN 1970, A CHEMISTRY LECTURER, known for his love of food, was asked if he wanted to run a café and a Liverpool institution was born. Paddy Burns, and partner David Scott, also from a chemistry background, set about building a team to run the Everyman Bistro, with the idea of using good quality ingredients to serve Mediterranean inspired fresh food in a place where people could socialise.

They started serving salads and dishes that could easily be reheated in microwaves, because they could not open during Everyman Theatre performances. The long queues waiting for them to open meant they had to be quick with service and strangely it's this style of food, born out of necessity, that is part of the café's continuing attraction. People began to perceive it as a vegetarian restaurant but it was simply that they wanted to move away from the traditional idea of 'meat and two veg'. At first they had to search far and wide for quality produce. Nowadays they find it much easier to source locally.

Everyman

The Everyman is surrounded by other quality restaurants along Hope Street, a far cry from the days when the area was something of a 'foodie' desert. At one end of Hope Street, the Catholic Cathedral has a new café that's already building customer loyalty.

At 60 Hope Street, locally-born chef Gary Manning has recreated one of Liverpool's famous foods – the deep-fried jam butty. The nineteenth century Carriageworks reopened in 2004 as a fine dining restaurant and hotel. Within the year it was recognised as the Newcomer of the Year in the *Sunday Times'* Best of British. Across the road Number Seven delicatessen, run by the Ainscough family, serves up the best produce from the North West and the UK, such as flavour intense bacon from Cumbria and buffalo cheese from Cheshire.

There is Blackburne House café, where food is sourced from local suppliers. Take a quick detour down a narrow alley off the main thoroughfare, knock on a door and you'll be admitted to a room filled with the wonderful aroma of coffee. Here Bellew's roasts coffee for sale across the region and you can buy straight from their door during the week, a real example of the many hidden culinary gems which Merseyside has to offer. Continue down the street past the suitcase sculpture and the renowned Liverpool Institute of Performing Arts and you come to the sandstone grandeur of the Anglican Cathedral, a perfect place to stop for a traditional English afternoon tea in spectacular surroundings.

i **Everyman Bistro, 13, Hope Street, Liverpool L1 9BH**
0151 708 9545

60 Hope Street, Liverpool L1 9BZ
0151 707 6060

The London Carriage Works, 40 Hope Street,
Liverpool L1 9DA
0151 705 2222 www.hopestreethotel.co.uk

Number Seven Deli, 15 Faulkner Street, Liverpool L8 7PU
0151 709 9633

Blackburne House, Blackburne Place, Hope Street,
Liverpool L8 7PE
0151 709 4356

Church Farm Organics

TEN YEARS AGO, when Steve Ledsham lost his job in the fire service, he looked at the 24 hectare farm near Thurstaston, Wirral and made a decision. The soil and the coastal situation were perfect for organic farming, so Steve and his family decided to follow their dream and start a farm. It seemed logical for them to go organic as they were averse to using chemicals and wanted a return to old fashioned farming methods.

But he knew that these days farmers have to supplement their income in other ways, so he opened a farm shop; a place where people could buy everything organic. His passion is infectious and he's extremely proud that over 80 per cent of the fresh produce he sells in the shop is from his farm.

When people buy his vegetables they can be guaranteed that they have not travelled more than a couple of hundred metres and were picked fresh from the ground just a few hours earlier. He sources other delicacies throughout the UK, bringing in the best quality foods such as the Patchwork Pates, Duchy Originals puddings and Scottish organic ice cream, as well as organic wines and beers.

Steve also runs a box scheme and his pleasant, purpose-built wooden shop includes a cosy tea and coffee bar offering sandwiches and cakes. His aim was

Church Farm

to become the best organic farm shop in the North West and his work was rewarded when it was voted Best Farm Shop in the UK in the 2004 Soil Association Organic Food Awards.

He also wants to educate future generations about the beneficial value of organics and hosts party and school visits to give children a taste of life on the farm. They even get a chance to dig up their own vegetables and take them home. Other ideas to keep people coming back include a lavender maze, and pumpkin and asparagus festivals, making Church Farm a satisfying visitor experience and not just a place to shop.

i **Church Farm Organics**
Church Lane, Thurstaston, Wirral CH61 0HW
0151 648 7838 www.churchfarm.org.uk

Wirral Farmers' Market

THINK OF FARMERS' MARKETS and you probably picture a rural setting, bustling crowds exploring brightly coloured stalls under open skies. Forget all that, one of Merseyside's best kept secrets is that its most popular farmers' market is not only indoors but is in a fairly urban area.

Since setting up three years ago Wirral Farmers' Market, held on the second Saturday of the month in New Ferry, has gone from strength to strength.

Around 2,000 to 3,000 customers come through the doors from all over the North West and as far away as North Wales to shop at the 35 different stalls.

Inside there's an old fashioned community feel as friends, neighbours and the regulars stop for a chat and a catch up over a cup of tea at the refreshment bar. Local bacon and black puddings come from Paul Ennion in Wirral and free range chickens from Lancashire. There's also olive oil from Spain courtesy of Wirralian Constanza Sweetman-Gamez. Even Ian Lloyd, who just sells eggs, has customers queueing up, anxious to pick up his legendary double yolkers.

Moist, delicious and just like mother used to make, cakes from Mary Walton are always a sell out, as are Carol Harvie's pies and soups all made from local produce. For those with a sweet tooth there are two chocolate, one confectionery and various cake stalls. For the healthy option there's fresh fish from Cumbria and vegetables harvested that morning.

Ready-prepared meals are the latest popular addition with Greek, Lebanese, French and Italian dishes on the menu. Most of the customers are regulars but more are discovering the market each month. Management of the market itself is unusual in that it is run completely by volunteers, who all have full time jobs, and run the market in their spare time.

It was established with three aims: to help regenerate the area; to bring sustainable fresh food to the local people; and to help producers, making it possibly unique among farmers' markets.

> ℹ **Wirral Farmers' Market**
> **Grove Street, New Ferry, Wirral**
> **0151 643 1393**
> The market is held on the second Saturday of the month.

Wapping Brewery

LIVERPOOL'S BALTIC TRIANGLE – the area of waterfront that used to deal in timber from the Baltic countries – is about to be transformed into a new residential and commercial district. All the speculative new plans, encouraged by Liverpool's upcoming City of Culture 2008 status, have one thing in common – they leave the Baltic Fleet pub, a listed Victorian building with a few Georgian bits here and there, exactly as it is. That is good news for all who enjoy real beer, for the Baltic Fleet is home to the Wapping Brewery.

Stan Shaw is head brewer, operating a small five-barrel plant in the cellars and secret smugglers' passageways beneath the pub. One passage went from

149

the pub under the road to the waterfront. The other one, a grim reminder of Liverpool's past, had manacles screwed into the wall.

The Wapping Brewery produces a bewildering variety of beers – Stan sent a dozen different brews to the last Liverpool Beer Festival. The repertoire includes Summer, a pale, straw-coloured beer which is on sale all the year round because it is Stan's favourite tipple. There is Wapping Bitter, a Stout (which some regard as much tastier than Guinness), a Weisse (wheat) beer and, strongest of all, Whopping Wapping, which Stan invented to celebrate his hundredth beer in the brewery in early 2004.

The Baltic Fleet is a landmark pub – it stocks excellent beers, its own as well as guest beers – and is justly famous for its food, especially the Sunday roast. And just to add to its delights, there isn't a television, jukebox, cigarette or fruit machine in sight. Altogether a remarkable success story, especially when you consider it was semi derelict and all but abandoned only six years ago.

  Baltic Fleet and Wapping Brewery
33 Wapping, Liverpool L1 8DQ
0151 709 3116

The Red Cat

Gastropub

ONLY A FEW MINUTES outside the urban sprawl of Liverpool and St Helens you suddenly take a sharp turn and find yourself in rural countryside. Cruise along country lanes and you come across a solid red brick pub, just like many others you might find in the region. But the Red Cat in Crank is a pub with a difference.

Inside, the décor is traditional with dark colours and a small bar – but look around the walls and clues start to emerge. Chalk boards list adventurous menus made from locally-sourced produce and there's a list of 'Classic European' and 'New World' wines including Bordeaux and Burgundies and some superstars from Chile, California and Australia.

Steve and Moira Calderbank have recently taken over this village pub. Steve's main mission is to reinstate it as the focal point of the local community. He says he aims to realize this by continuing the Red Cat's already popular status as a great pub with great food and great people.

The Red Cat now provides bar meals, Sunday lunches, an early diner offer and a full à la carte menu. Where possible, food is sourced locally, with

vegetables coming from local farms and menus changing with the seasons and day by day, depending on what they can find.

In spring, Bowland lamb and pork and Formby asparagus make a welcome appearance. Duck and chicken are sourced from Goosnargh and game comes from the shoots that take place around Crank in the autumn. Dishes could include a salad of smoked salmon, asparagus wrapped in pancetta, herbed cream cheese; partridge and roast figs in balsamic red sauce, or grilled sea bass with mussels, prawns, cream sauce and fine noodles.

Featured in practically every UK pub guide, The Red Cat won the *Morning Advertiser* Regional Best Food Pub of the Year for the North in 2004 and then went on to win the national prize. People travel from all over the region to enjoy head chef Gavin Richardson's food and though it's best to book ahead, you can be guaranteed the warmest of welcomes, fantastic wines and excellent food.

The Red Cat
8 Red Cat Lane, Crank, St Helens WA11 8RU
01744 882422

Marc Verité
The Warehouse Brasserie

SINCE OPENING IN 1996, the Warehouse Brasserie has established itself both as one of the best restaurants on Merseyside and as a champion of locally produced food. Chef director Marc Verité, trained at Southport College, but has worked in some of the top restaurants of Belgium and France.

Marc's policy of sourcing local produce includes not just the fruit and vegetables, which come from the market gardens of West Lancashire and Merseyside, but as much meat and fish as possible. Typical of this is the use of sea bass in the restaurant. Rather than use farmed sea bass from Spain or Greece, Marc prefers locally caught sea bass which has fed on natural food, as have the shrimps he uses from the local Southport shrimp fishery.

Since opening, the Warehouse Brasserie has steadily collected a string of critical awards, including being featured in *The Good Food Guide 2004*, a Bib Gourmand Award in the *Michelin Restaurant Guide*, which the restaurant has held for three years, and *AA Restaurant Guide* rosettes.

The Brasserie's chefs have also collected individual awards. Ben Whitley was named Best Young Chef in Merseyside 2003, while in 2002 the Brasserie's head chef, Darren Smith, scooped the North West Young Chef of the Year title, as well as the Best Young Chef in Merseyside Award. Anthony Greenland won Best Young Chef in Merseyside 2004.

i **The Warehouse Brasserie**
30 West Street, Southport PR8 1QN
01704 544662 www.warehouse-brasserie.co.uk

Amy Cook

Roasted wild sea bass on grilled Formby asparagus served with spiced Southport shrimp butter.

Merseyside Recipe Roasted Wild Sea Bass on Grilled Formby Asparagus served with Spiced Southport Shrimp Butter

Serves 4

What you need

4 large fillets of wild sea bass, skin on, scaled, pin-boned
2 bunches of Formby asparagus
12oz Southport peeled shrimps
1tsp chopped chives
Pinch of mace
Pinch of cayenne pepper
Dash of Tabasco sauce
Finely grated zest of half a lemon
Salt to taste
250g of softened unsalted farmhouse butter
4 small bunches of baby plum vine tomatoes
2tbsp of balsamic vinegar syrup (reduced balsamic vinegar)

What you do

Shrimp Butter

Beat the softened butter with the mace, cayenne pepper, lemon zest, chopped chives and Tabasco sauce. Then fold in the shrimps with a touch of salt to taste. Place on a sheet of greaseproof paper. Wrap the paper around the butter to create a sausage shape. Place in the fridge and leave to set.

Asparagus and Tomatoes

Using a peeler, peel the asparagus from half way down the stem towards the white bulky end. Trim the peeled asparagus down leaving around three to four inches with the tip.

To grill, roll the asparagus tips in a little olive oil and season with salt and pepper. Place on a pre-heated griddle pan and sear for three to four minutes on each side. Remove from griddle and keep warm. For the vine tomatoes, cook as the asparagus and keep warm.

Roasted Wild Sea Bass

In a very hot non-stick frying pan, place the oiled and seasoned sea bass fillets skin side down and leave to colour for a couple of minutes.

When coloured, turn them over and place in a hot oven (180°C) for a further 3-4 minutes. Remove from pan and leave to stand in a warm place.

To present the dish

Place the asparagus tips in the centre of the plate, place the sea bass on top with the tomatoes to the side. Drizzle some balsamic syrup around the plate. To finish, put a slice of shrimp butter on top of the sea bass and serve immediately.

CHEF'S TIPS

- The spiced shrimps can be made in advance and can be stored in the fridge for up to a week.
- It's important to use unsalted butter for the shrimps as there is salt naturally present in the shrimps.
- Formby asparagus is only in season for a short time, from mid-April to the end of June, but I believe it is the best asparagus you can buy.
- Leaving the skin on the fish helps prevent it breaking up during cooking and presenting the fish skin side upwards makes an attractive dish. The skin will just pull off with a knife and fork.
- The balsamic vinegar syrup sounds strong, but by using a good quality vinegar, you concentrate the natural sugars. The sharpness of the vinegar complements the slightly oily nature of sea bass.

CHESHIRE

Stride this county, cycle, ride and rail it
And like that map unfold it north to south
East to west – canal it, cross it, trail it
Roll it in your eyes, taste it in your mouth

Step into Cheshire by John Lindley
Cheshire Poet Laureate 2004

CHESHIRE

THE PICTURESQUE LANDSCAPE OF THE CHESHIRE REGION is characterised by lowland plains, woodlands, river valleys and meres. Rich farmland is interspersed with woods and hedges, green parkland and an intricate network of canals that meander through the lush countryside. The county is composed of market towns, villages and hamlets, dotted with stunning black and white timbered houses.

Although there are arable farms along with beef and sheep farming, historically, the Cheshire region is primarily a dairy farming area – the thick glacial drift of clays and sands deposited during the last Ice Age, resulted in soils ideally suited to pasture. The rich Cheshire soil contains a variety of minerals, including salt, which was originally worked by the ancient Romans. The salt deposits beneath the soil of the Cheshire Plain gave rise to salt works and spas such as Nantwich. Cheshire is the only place in Britain where salt is still produced on a large scale.

The salt deposits, together with the many grasses, herbs and flowers that flourish in the soil and grazing pastures, impart a unique flavour to the region's high quality milk – and thus the celebrated Cheshire cheese, which has a salty tang and a hint of herbal grassiness. Cheshire cheese is England's oldest recorded cheese and was mentioned in the *Domesday Book*. The plentiful supply of milk has also produced several other spin-off products such as rich dairy ice cream and yoghurt.

Cheshire's small specialist food producers are dedicated to producing high quality foods and employ their skills using traditional time honoured methods. This benefits both customers and producers; consumers receive fresh nutritious local produce and the reassurance of knowing where the food comes from and producers receive a fair price for their food.

The farmers and growers who produce these foods are craftsmen and women – they know their animals; they choose varieties of fruit and vegetables for flavour, not appearance; cheesemakers make cheese by hand for optimum flavour. Everything is produced with care and commitment and there are no short cuts. The result is food at its best, at the peak of freshness and packed with deep rich flavours – something sadly missing from the often completely tasteless commercially mass-produced offerings.

The skill, passion and dedication of Cheshire's food producers is reflected in the many award-winning products that flow from the county farms, dairies, bakeries and homely cafés.

Katie Reiley, owner of the marton Coffee House in Congleton, epitomises the enterprise shown by the specialist producer. Her restaurant customers have been so enthusiastic about her handmade dishes that she has now branched out into ready-made meals under the 'Natural Larder' brand. Her moussaka dish, made to her own recipe with local ingredients, won the Best Ready Meal Award in the 2004 Producer of the Year Awards, a competition organised by North West Fine Foods and sponsored by Booths as part of the British Food Fortnight.

Other awards underline the quality, craftsmanship and often adventurous, nature of Cheshire's food heroes. The county demonstrated its skill in cheesemaking – a tradition that dates back to 186 AD – by capturing two awards. The Traditional Regional Speciality Award went to HS Bourne of Malpas, for its Cheshire cheese, whilst Ravens Oak Dairy at Nantwich collected the Best Cheese and Overall Best Dairy accolade with its Whitehaven goat cheese.

It is not just in signature foods that Cheshire makes its mark. The Haworth family of Eddisbury Fruit Farm, Kelsall, captured the Best Soft Drinks Award for their Blackcurrant and Apple juice (made with 100 per cent pure apple juice) and The Baker in Gatley, scooped the award for Best Overall Dessert with a chocolate tart made with the intensely-flavoured Valhona chocolate. The Bakery is a new venture for award-winning chef Duncan Poyser, who makes artisan breads and patisseries, and highlights the ambition and willingness of many young people across the region to invest time, money and energy in specialist food business.

These producers are not content to rest on their laurels; they ensure they keep up with new trends by offering more exotic and newly fashionable foods such as wild boar, ostrich and buffalo cheese. Visitors, bon viveurs and ordinary consumers alike will find a splendid choice of food and drink in the county's farm shops, farmers' markets, pubs, delicatessens and even stalls at the roadside – an encouraging sign of a thriving food culture and a growing market for food produced with concern for animal welfare and the environment.

Cheshire's specialist food producers enjoy the support of the Duke of Westminster, who is president of Made in Cheshire, a partnership of Cheshire County Council, local producers and district councils.

Cheshire Cheese

CHRIS WADE OF MOLLINGTON, near Chester, makes cheeses by hand using raw milk from local farms on the saltbeds of the Cheshire Plain. His cheeses – Cheshire (red, white and blue), Red Leicester, Double Gloucester and Sage Derby are available locally and from Fortnum and Mason under the Mollington Farms label. He also supplies a wholesaler and his cheeses are sold in Waitrose.

He uses traditional methods without preservatives and never makes block cheese, but traditional wheels of varying sizes, each carefully wrapped in cloth to allow the cheese to breathe and mature.

Chris sells his cheeses when young – anywhere from six weeks to four months, as these have the best flavour. Red Leicester is the most popular cheese and he is the only cheesemaker to make this using non-pasteurised milk. His latest product is a rich tasting creamy Blue Cheshire, a revival of a connoisseur's cheese last made in the 1980s. Proof of the quality of his cheeses lies in the numerous national and international awards he has won.

HS Bourne at Malpas, another artisan producer and winner of the Traditional Regional Speciality Award in the 2004 North West Producer of the Year Competition, also turns out an impressive range of Cheshire cheeses using the traditional 'hands-on' techniques. Their award-winners include Mrs Bourne's Mature Cheshire; John Bourne's Organic Cheshire; Oak Smoked Cheshire and Blue Cheshire. There are also seasonal specials and organic butter.

HS Bourne

The milk used to make the cheese comes from their pedigree Holstein Friesian cows. The milk for the organic cheese is produced on a farm in Cheshire. That farm and the cheese dairy have the Certificate of Approval issued by the Association of Organic Farmers and Growers. Bourne's aim is to produce cheeses closer in flavour and texture to the great Cheshires of the past, than to the modern industrially processed cheese, which is mild and crumbly. After making, the cheeses are stored for up to 12 months to ensure that they fully mature, resulting in an old fashioned rich tangy flavour.

Their cheese is available at farmers' markets nationwide including the famous Borough Market in Southwark, direct from their farm and also by mail order.

i **Mollington Farms Ltd**
Grange Farm, Mollington, Cheshire CH1 6NP
01244 851 982 www.mollington-cheese.co.uk

HS Bourne, The Bank, Malpas, Cheshire SY14 7AL
01948 770214 www.hsbourne.co.uk

Cholmondeley Castle Farm Shop

LONGHORN CATTLE HAVE THE DISTINCTION of being the oldest traditional breed in Britain and the ones that made the 'roast beef of olde England' famous. They are now classified as a rare breed.

Cholmondeley's herd of 60 Longhorns were born and reared in the traditional way on the estate, grazing peacefully on herbal pasture rich in wild flowers. Farm manager Mike Allman attributes the meat's distinctive deep flavour and velvety texture to the fact that the cattle are entirely grass fed and allowed to mature slowly.

The cattle are killed quickly after the short journey to the local slaughterhouse. This means the animals are not stressed in any way, an important factor in the tenderness of the meat. All the meat is fully traceable and after slaughter is hung for ten days.

The intense flavour and fine-grained texture of the meat made it a winner of the Made in Cheshire Rural Enterprise of the Year. Food writer Clarissa Dickson Wright has described it as 'the best flavoured beef I have ever come across'.

Longhorn beef is only sold in the estate's well-stocked farm shop, a further incentive to visit the castle. As well as joints and steak, the beef is used for a filling

Award-Winning Producer

for the delicious pies that are also sold in the shop. Unfortunately demand easily exceeds supply but estate manager James Hall has plans to increase the size of the herd and hopes to supply local restaurants in the near future.

 Cholmondeley Castle Farm Shop
Cholmondeley, Malpas SY14 8AQ
01829 720203

Cheshire Farm Ice Cream

TOM AND MARGARET FELL began producing their award-winning dairy ice cream in 1986 and have never looked back. Smooth, rich and creamy, Cheshire Farm ice cream contains nothing artificial whatsoever and is made with only fresh milk, double cream and top quality ingredients.

The milk comes from the farm and is made into ice cream within 24 hours of milking. The herd is Freedom Food accredited, fed on a totally natural diet and all the milk is fully traceable. Their ice cream has won a host of awards including Silver for the Rhubarb and Custard flavour and Bronze for the

Cheshire Farm and NWFF

Chocolate ice cream at the Great Taste Awards 2003. The Great Taste Awards 2004 proved even more successful with Gold for their Vanilla ice cream.

There are 30 flavours, but the top sellers are Vanilla, speckled with vanilla pod seeds and Honeycomb, with chunks of dark cinder toffee. Mint Choc Chip and Banana are the top two children's favourites. The latest flavour is Liquorice and Blackcurrant. There's also a choice of mouth-watering real fruit sorbets including Pink Grapefruit and Mango and Ginger. Flavours change all the time and seasonal specials such as Christmas Pudding are often added to the range.

Staff are happy for customers to sample the ice cream before they buy and as well as the ever popular cones, you can buy any flavour in the distinctive white, gold and black tubs to take home in an insulated cool bag. Visitors can sit and enjoy their ice cream at a table in the ice cream parlour and watch the ice cream being made 'live' on the television screen, by the small team of skilled workers. There is also a gift shop and tearoom serving excellent lunches and afternoon teas.

The farm has the capacity to produce 20,000 litres of ice cream per hour and it is supplied to major airlines such as Air Atlanta and Air Canada, in addition to many hotels, restaurants and retail outlets.

i **Cheshire Farm Ice Cream**
Newton Lane, Tattenhall, Chester CH3 9NE
01829 770995 www.cheshirefarmicecream.co.uk

Drink

Cheshire Apple Juice

COLIN HAWORTH WAS BORN ON THE FARM and has continued the family tradition with great success. He grows a variety of fruits including apples (26 varieties no less), pears and summer berries. Apart from the better-known apple varieties such as Bramley and Gala, there are also lesser-known old fashioned varieties such as St Edmunds Pippin and Ashmeads Kernel, which was first grown in 1700.

Colin's stepson and business partner, Michael Dykes, started to bottle the apple juice, beginning with single variety Cox and Bramley. Now around 16 apple varieties are pressed to produce juice, including Kidd's Orange (an old variety) and Russet. The farm produces 50,000 bottles annually including a popular blend of Blackcurrant and Apple Juice, which earned the accolade of the Best Soft Drink in the 2004 North West Producer of the Year Awards. The drink is made from the juices of Spartan and Jona-go-red apples and Ben Loman blackcurrant varieties.

The apple juice is completely natural; all that is added is a little Vitamin C as an anti-oxidant. The freshly pressed juice is pasteurised and bottled and has a two year shelf life. There is also a new sweetened Raspberry Juice.

A recent innovation has been the introduction of more specialised apple juices – Apple and Vanilla, Apple and Cinnamon and Apple and Ginger, which are very popular. In winter the cinnamon and ginger are heated and served (an ideal warming alternative to mulled wine for drivers and children) at the many farmers' markets where Colin and his wife Monica sell their juices.

Cider is also made on the farm and Michael has a drinks licence to sell the cider, either from the barrel, or ready bottled. A recent development is a range of fruit wines, including Tayberry, Rhubarb and Gooseberry.

> *i* **Eddisbury Fruit Farm**
> **Yeld Lane, Kelsall, Cheshire CW6 0TE**
> **01829 751255 www.eddisbury.co.uk**

The Cheshire Smokehouse

The Cheshire Smokehouse

THE CHESHIRE SMOKEHOUSE AT MORLEY GREEN, Wilmslow, which is owned and run by John and Darren Ward, is a well laid out treasure house of fine food from around the world and also includes a café, patisserie and wine department.

The smokehouse itself is behind the shop. Here, ham, bacon, turkey, chicken, duck, trout, salmon, mackerel, kippers, cheeses, nuts and, most recently, peppers, are smoked over smouldering oak, maple or hickory wood, according to the product. The Hickory Smoked nuts are addictive and are supplied to Waitrose and Lakeland Ltd. Smoking foods is an art that has been in the family since 1907, when John Ward's grandfather started a small bacon smoking business in Manchester on his return from working in Canada.

Produce and raw ingredients are sourced locally whenever possible and all the meat is completely traceable. Everything is chosen with quality in mind and the choice is breathtaking. There's a wonderful selection of traditional bacon – Dry-cured; Sweet Black (cured with molasses), Canadian (John's grandfather brought the recipe back from Canada) and Honey-cured. They also make their own sausages (fresh and smoked) and patés. Their Baked Cheshire Ham glazed with honey and muscovado sugar excels.

Pastries, cakes and a tempting array of breads, including specialities such as sourdough and ciabatta, are made fresh every day in the small bakery behind the shop. Whatever you're looking for you're sure to find it in this attractive shop – artisan cheeses, chocolates, olives, a range of freshly made frozen dishes such as lasagne and Dauphinoise potatoes. A new addition to the shop is a range of herbs from a local herb farm.

About nine years ago the Smokehouse café was opened, serving meals and snacks and has since won prizes for the quality and innovation of its food and menu. The wine department is run by Philip Beavan who is very knowledgeable about all the wines stocked – over 400 at the last count! All the wines come from traditional small producers, many of whom are family owned. Philip is very happy to advise customers on which wines to choose.

The Cheshire Smokehouse has won many awards, including the title Best Ham and Bacon in Britain from Henrietta Green in her book *The Foodlovers Guide to Britain*; the shop also won the coveted BBC Good Food Award for Best Speciality Shop in the UK for 1999-2000.

i **The Cheshire Smokehouse**
Vost Farm, Morley Green, Wilmslow SK9 5NU
01625 548499 www.cheshiresmokehouse.co.uk

Le Chocolatier

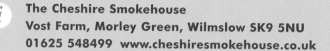

BASED IN GREAT BARROW, NEAR CHESTER, Michael Levy gave up a lucrative career as an accountant to pursue his passion for chocolate and is now a chocolatier par excellence. He started his business, Le Chocolatier, in 1993 in his home kitchen. The biggest problem at the time was learning about chocolate, so he contacted some chocolate specialists and soon developed a network of contacts around Europe who proved to be both expert and willing to help him.

Le Chocolatier

Michael Levy's unique handmade chocolates are delectable and probably among the best you'll ever taste. He supplies chocolates to high-class food stores (Fortnum and Mason, Selfridges, Harrods) as well as by mail order.

All the chocolates are made with the highest quality continental couvertures and, in line with the finest Swiss and Belgian chocolates, they have a very high proportion of cocoa-solids and definitely no vegetable fats, artificial preservatives or colours. Only the freshest and highest quality ingredients are used, eg fresh double cream, unsalted Normandy butter and natural flavours like honey, lemon and caramel.

The truffles are rolled individually and one of the most popular is the Bitter Chocolate Truffle made with fresh cream, butter and chocolate (74% cocoa solids). Chocoholics are also offered intriguingly flavoured chocolates such as Nutmeg Cream, Earl Grey Tea and Whisky and Chocolate Mousse.

The latest products include a new range of fresh cream chocolates made with double cream and cocoa nibs (roasted chopped cocoa beans), which are excellent when baking cookies, cakes, etc for a deep chocolate flavour, as well as 'Atkins friendly' chocolates which are also suitable for diabetics. These are discs of very low carbohydrate, sugar-free chocolate topped with roasted macadamias, pecans and hazelnuts.

When he's not making chocolates, Michael also offers The Chocolate Experience. This includes the history of chocolate and how it's made, plus the chance to sample real cocoa beans and a great number of outstanding chocolates. This is very popular and many hotels, corporate entertainment companies and charities are among his customers.

i **Le Chocolatier**
8 Barrow Estate, Great Barrow, Chester CH3 7JA
01829 741010 www.cocoasolid.com

The Housekeeper's Store at Tatton Park

THE HOUSEKEEPER'S STORE in the Stableyard at Tatton Park is an Aladdin's cave for lovers of good food. The shop stocks an impressive selection of high quality food from around Britain, together with fine produce from the Tatton Home Farm and Estate and choice foods from local small producers.

Tatton's own produce includes a range of superb venison from the ancient parkland and hand-cured bacon from the Park's own rare breed pigs. Tatton's association with deer dates back to ancient times. The herds of Red and Fallow deer graze freely across the estate's parkland as they have done for centuries. During the winter they are given a supplementary feed of carrots and hay. The Store offers sliced smoked venison, cured in port, juniper berries and herbs, then hot smoked over oak chippings by a local family firm. The venison is classed as prime venison and is young, tender and low in fat, and therefore does not require hanging or marinating. Many local chefs include Tatton Prime Venison on their menus. There's a variety of cuts on offer – from hand-diced (best for casseroles or stews) to steaks and joints. There's also tasty potted venison.

Hebridean sheep also graze on the parkland and are part of Tatton's history. The rare breed lamb is naturally reared to produce a finely grained and well-flavoured meat.

Tatton's six-acre walled gardens have been skilfully restored to their pre-First World War state and now once again yield a wonderful selection of old fashioned varieties of fruit and vegetables, nourished with manure from the Home Farm. The tomato, orchid and fig houses have all been rebuilt to the original designs and there's a mushroom house, as well as an onion loft and fruit stores. There are also courses that should help to revive almost forgotten horticultural processes and traditional gardening skills.

(i) **The Housekeeper's Store**
Tatton Park, Knutsford, Cheshire WA16 6QN
01625 534422 www.tattonpark.org.uk

Holly Tree Farm Shop

The Bluecoat Press

KAROL BAILEY STARTED HOLLY TREE FARM SHOP at Tabley, Knutsford, in 1989 and sells a splendid selection of beef, pork, lamb and mutton (increasingly hard to find nowadays) including rare breeds and poultry. There are good meaty sausages made from pork and/or turkey; and a small but excellent selection of British cheeses, such as Long Clawson Stilton and Stinking Bishop, along with farmhouse butter.

Karol is particularly renowned for her high quality turkeys and geese and is known locally as 'The Goose Woman'. Goose sells particularly well in autumn and at Christmas and Karol fast freezes a few for last minute customers. She also sells cartons of goose fat (it makes the best roast potatoes) and goose grease with aromatherapy oils to soothe cracked heels and skin complaints. Goose eggs are available and sold blown, ready to decorate.

Turkeys, although especially popular at Christmas, are sold all year round and as turkey joints, burgers and steaks. All the meat and poultry in the shop – whether fresh or frozen – comes from free range animals fed on a completely natural diet free from additives and antibiotics. Everything is traceable; Karol knows exactly from which animals her meat comes and she is a Rare Breeds Accredited Butcher.

She's a keen cook and this is evident in the shop's range of delicious preserves and chutneys (made with whatever fruits and vegetables are in season); meaty sausage rolls, mouth-watering pies and tempting cakes and scones.

The shop also stocks a good choice of bottle-conditioned real ales, English wines and liqueurs, including an unusual Ginger Dry Sherry – with pieces of ginger root – perfect accompaniment for Chinese dishes. Karol hosts several gourmet events throughout the year – dinners, cookery demonstrations, tastings etc, which are very popular.

Holly Tree Farm Shop
Chester Road, Tabley, Knutsford WA16 0EU
01565 651835 www.hollytreefarmshop.co.uk

Nantwich Farmers' Market

The Bluecoat Press

A BUSTLING FARMERS' MARKET is held in the town square on the last Saturday of each month in the charming and historic market town of Nantwich, where the impressive black and white listed buildings date back to the fourteenth century. The market was the first of its kind in Cheshire when opened in 1999 and has proved very popular with both the public and food producers, attracting around 4,000 visitors every month.

Nantwich is widely regarded as one of the best farmers' markets in Britain and together with the town's Food Festival and Food Directory, won a Gold trophy in the 2003 Green Apple Awards, after being cited as amongst the very best examples of support for local farmers and retailers in the country.

According to the season there are 23-28 stalls, with more in the summer as more produce becomes available. There's an admirable selection of produce, including organic foods. Top quality meat, includes ostrich and wild boar, organic herbs including an unusual caraway mint, delicious breads (Scarborough Fair loaf contains parsley, sage, rosemary and thyme), homemade cakes, tasty pies, fresh fish, farm cheeses and butter and a great range of sausages.

The atmosphere is pleasant and friendly, with producers eager to answer questions and chat about their products. Prices are reasonable and the food is fresh and of top quality. After filling your shopping bags you can go in search of refreshment in the wide choice of cafés, pubs and restaurants in the town.

i **Nantwich Farmers' Market**
The Square, Nantwich
01270 537805
The market is held on the last Saturday in the month.

The Old Creamery Bottling Company

THEN KNOWN AS THE PARADISE BREWERY, the company opened for business in 2000 in a former creamery just a short stroll from Wrenbury railway station and a longer stride from the Llangollen Canal. John Wood and his then partner used to run a business involving the recycling of plastics, but decided a brewery on the same site might be a better bet.

There's always been a bar attached, with limited hours, for bona fide

Micro Brewery

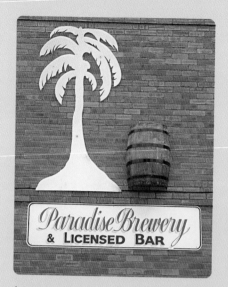

brewery visitors – John was recently granted a normal pub licence after promising to remove the sawdust to 'enhance the ambience' of the place, a move not altogether approved of by aficionados. However, you can now visit and drink for a couple of hours each weekday evening and for normal pub hours over the weekend. It might be a good idea to ring and confirm those hours before making a trip from a distance.

John brews a variety of beers, but the most popular by far is Marbury Mild, which makes up 80 per cent of his total production. All the pundits would have you believe that mild is out of fashion – obviously, nobody told Cheshire beer enthusiasts.

John also masterminds a couple of unusual beer festivals each year. One takes place in an otherwise quiet period between Christmas and New Year, the other happens on the first weekend in July, to coincide with Wrenbury's Scarecrow Festival, when every garden in the village parades a scarecrow. On both occasions, the Manchester to Cardiff express is persuaded to stop at Wrenbury, so that far-flung fans can come by train. There are further rewards – John selects other beers from local breweries, not just his own portfolio and just up the road is one of Cheshire's most famous real-ale pubs, the Bhurtpore Inn.

 The Old Creamery Bottling Company
Paradise Brewery, The Old Creamery, Wrenbury,
Cheshire CW5 8EX
01270 780916

The Dysart Arms

THE DYSART ARMS EPITOMISES THE CLASSIC ENGLISH VILLAGE PUB, with bookcases, lots of old oak, old photographs and a pleasant garden. Liz and Darren Snell have run this magnificent pub for almost six years and have won many awards including the *Good Pub Guide*'s Cheshire Dining Pub of the Year 2004 Award, the *Which Guide to Country Pubs 2004* Award and the *Good Beer Guide (CAMRA)* Rural Pub of the Year 2003 Award.

The head chef is Warren Davies who devised the tempting menu (this changes every two months) which includes local produce such as Bunbury bangers with mash and onion gravy and a tasty Ploughman's of Shropshire Blue, Beeston Cheshire and pork pie, served with crusty bread, apple, celery and chutney. Puddings include much loved stalwarts such as Warren's dark, sweet (but not sickly sweet) treacle tart.

The cheeseboard boasts a selection of fine British farmhouse cheeses such as handmade Blue Stilton and Brindley Buffalo, a soft creamy cheese made from organic milk. The wine list is reasonably priced and there's also a splendid choice of real ale and Irish and Scotch malt whiskies. The staff are efficient, helpful and friendly and very knowledgeable about the dishes on the menu.

i **The Dysart Arms**
Bowes Gate Road, Bunbury, Near Tarporley CW9 6PH
01829 260183 www.dysartarms-bunbury.co.uk

The Dysart Arms

The Chester Grosvenor

Simon Radley
The Arkle Restaurant

TO EARN A STAR FROM THE HIGHLY RATED *Michelin Guide* is hard, but any chef who achieves this accolade will admit that keeping the star for the restaurant is even harder. There are regular inspections and the slightest slip-up can see the star removed.

Simon Radley, executive chef of the Arkle Restaurant and the Chester Grosvenor Hotel, has kept the cooking and service so polished and imaginative that the Arkle has held its Michelin star for 14 years.

He started at the Chester Grosvenor in 1986 as a junior chef, rising to head chef in 1993. Soon after, Simon moved to another star-rated hotel to further develop his culinary skills, but returned in 1998 to be executive head chef, the position he holds today.

i **The Arkle Restaurant**
The Chester Grosvenor Hotel, Chester CH1 1LT
01244 324024 www.chestergrosvenor.co.uk

Amy Cook

Cheshire beef with ox cheek pudding and seasonal vegetables.

Cheshire Recipe Cheshire Beef with Ox Cheek Pudding and Seasonal Vegetables

Serves 4

What you need

Main dish

800g single piece of Cheshire beef fillet steak
1kg of ox cheek
1 carrot
1 leek
1 stick of celery
1 onion
1 bulb garlic
2 bay leaves
Sprig of thyme
2 litres good beef stock
100ml red wine
100ml port

For the Suet Pastry

4 small moulds or ramekins
125g plain flour
1 tsp baking powder
125g fresh white breadcrumbs
125g beef suet minced
Milk to bind
Pinch of salt

What you do

Finely chop the vegetables, seal and brown the ox cheeks in a lightly-oiled frying pan. Add the vegetables and caramelise them so they have a nutty appearance.

Tip off any excess fat, turn up the heat, add the red wine and port and stir so that the liquid captures any of the meat and vegetable juices on the bottom of the pan.

Transfer the meat and the juice from the frying pan to a covered casserole dish, add the bay leaves, thyme and beef stock. Cook in a low heat oven (145-150°C) for approximately three to four hours, or until there is no resistance when prodded with a finger or a fork.

Remove the ox cheek and cool on a tray. Pass the cooking liquid through a fine sieve into a clean pan, bring up to a steady simmer, skimming off all fat and scum while slowly reducing to about half the original amount.

For the suet pastry, combine flour, breadcrumb, suet, salt and baking powder, then bind together with a little cold milk to make a moist, pliable dough. Rest the pastry in the fridge for an hour.

Tear off at least 12 inches of cling film and line the ramekin moulds leaving a lot of overhang. Repeat with a second layer of cling film (this will make lifting the pudding out of the mould very easy).

Roll out the pastry dough on a floured surface. The amount of pastry you need for each ramekin depends on the size, but a typical 3 inch ramekin will need a piece eight inches square to line the ramekin with enough overhanging spare pastry to fold over the top to seal and complete the pudding. Press the pastry into the shape of the mould.

When the ox cheek reduction is to the required consistency, check the seasoning, remove from heat and slightly chill.

Break the ox cheek into one-inch pieces with your fingers and pour over enough of the cooking liquid to give a good gravy, but not too wet. Gently mix as you add the liquid.

Fill the pastry-lined moulds, fold over the overhanging pastry and ensure a good seal. Fold over the cling film and scrunch it together. A piece of string or wire bag tie will hold it in place. Keep in the fridge until the following day.

To present the dish

Steam puddings for one hour, depending on size and keep warm.

Season the beef fillet with salt and pepper and cook the beef in a hot oven to how you like steak – rare or well done. Rest the cooked beef in a warm place or covered with foil for at least 15 minutes so the juices flow back into the meat and it tenderises a little more.

Lift a pudding out of the ramekin with the cling film and place on the plate. Cut the beef into four thick slices and place a slice on top of a pudding.

Serve with creamed potatoes and a selection of seasonal vegetables.

CHEF'S TIPS

- The puddings are the most time consuming part of the recipe, but you can make them the day before and store them in the fridge to cook the following day.

- Ox cheek can be ordered through a good local butcher.

- To chill down the ox cheek cooking liquid, place the pan in a sink or bowl with cold water around the pan. Occasionally stir the liquid and change the water when it gets warm.

Further Information

Addresses and contact details for producers and retailers of local foods across the North West. Winners from the 2004 Producer of the Year Awards are highlighted in colour for each county.

180 – 189 **CUMBRIA**

189 – 197 **LANCASHIRE**

198 – 200 **GREATER MANCHESTER**

200 – 204 **MERSEYSIDE**

204 – 211 **CHESHIRE**

Northwest Fantastic Foods Partnership
Contact: Lorna Tyson
Rural Business Centre
Myerscough College
Bilsbarrow
Preston PR3 0RY
01995 642 255
ltyson@myerscough.ac.uk
www.nwfantasticfoods.co.uk

North West Fine Foods
Contact: Catherine Smith
West Lancashire Technology Management Centre
Moss Lane View
Skelmersdale
Lancashire WN8 9TN
01695 732 734
info@nwff.co.uk
www.nwff.co.uk

CUMBRIA

Made in Cumbria
Contact: John Anderson
County Offices, Busher Walk,
Kendal LA9 4RQ
01539 732 736
food@madeincumbria.co.uk
www.madeincumbria.co.uk

DAIRY AND EGGS

Artisan Ice Creams
50a Main Street, Kirby Lonsdale, Cumbria LA6 2AJ
015242 73324
Homemade ice cream and café.

Buttermere Ayrshires
Skye Farm, Buttermere, Cockermouth,
Cumbria CA13 9XA
017687 70277
louisekyle@ukf.net
Farm made ice cream, produced on the working
farm, using milk and cream from their own Ayrshire
cows.

Cream of Cumbria
Howberry, Blackford, Carlisle, Cumbria CA6 4EN
01228 675558
tomsusan@forrester32.fsnet.co.uk
Traditionally made butter from pasteurised cream.
Homemade scones, gingerbreads, cakes and pies.
Cooked pies using locally bred Aberdeen Angus
beef.

Cumbrian Maid
Dalegarth, Mascelles, Lindal in Furness,
Ulverston LA12 0TQ
01229 462909
cumbrianmaid@aol.com
Healthy frozen yoghurt blended with a selection of
fruits (blackcurrants, gooseberries and raspberries),
grown by the family on Cumbrian soil in organic
conditions.

David Knipe
Gateside Cottage, Levens, Kendal,
Cumbria LA8 8NL
015395 60287
knipesmilk@aol.com
Eggs, fresh barn and poultry.

English Lakes Ice Cream Ltd
The Old Dairy, Gilthwaiterigg Lane, Kendal,
Cumbria LA9 6NT
01539 721211
www.lakesicecream.com
Best Ice Cream Award Winner 2004 for
Cappucino. Dairy (Processed). A family run
firm. All products are natural, without artificial
flavours or colours.

Hartleys Ice Cream
24 Church Street, Egremont, Cumbria CA22 2AW
01946 820456
Homemade ice creams and sorbets.

Holme Farm Dairy Ice Cream
Holme Farm, Meathop Road,
Grange over Sands LA11 6QX
015395 32991
d.lawrence@meathop.ndo.co.uk
A family run dairy farm. Ice cream made using milk
from their herd of 120 black and white cows.

Lakeland Free Range Eggs
Bannerigg Farm, Windermere, Cumbria LA23 1JL
015394 43362
bannerigg@whsmithnet.co.uk
Free range eggs available at supermarkets, shops,
hotels and pubs, restaurants and delicatessens.
Also available from the farm gate.

Lakes Free Range Egg Company
Meg Bank, Stainton, Penrith, Cumbria CA11 0EE
01768 890460
Quality free range eggs to RSPCA Freedom Foods
welfare standards.

Springbank Free Range Poultry
Springbank Farm, High Walton, St Bees,
Cumbria CA22 2TY
01946 822375
stevewoodman@talk21.com
Free range eggs. Accredited unit with Rare Breed
Survival Trust for Scots Dumpy hens and other
breeds available. Also Portland sheep. Homebaking
and preserves from farm produce available at
farmers' markets.

Thornby Moor Dairy
Crofton Hall, Thursby, Carlisle, Cumbria CA5 6QB
016973 45555
leonie@ukf.net
Using unpasteurised milk from local goats and
shorthorn cows. Handmade cheeses relying on
traditional methods of production and maturation.

FRUIT AND VEGETABLES

Distington Victorian Walled Garden Association
Gilgarran Road, Distington, Workington,
Cumbria CA14 4QY
01946 834645
www.dvwg.co.uk
A community restoration and training garden, with New Deal trainees learning commercial horticulture. Producers and sellers of a large range of plants, herbs, vegetables and fruit (raspberries, redcurrants and asparagus). A range of homemade jams and chutneys.

Hill Crest
Cardewlees, Carlisle, Cumbria CA5 6LE
01228 710202
johnjoyw@aol.com
Fresh vegetables. Produce is picked on the day of sale. Crops are traditionally grown.

TH and J Graham
Manor House, Gamelsby, Wigton,
Cumbria CA7 0NX
016973 42687
Potatoes and vegetables.

BAKERY AND CONFECTIONERY

Ayleside Bakery
Glen View Farm, Ayle, Alston, Cumbria CA9 3NH
01434 381898
margaret@glenview01.freeserve.co.uk
Range of loaves: banana and honey, sticky loaf, apricot hazelnut, ginger and orange. Scones and tray bakes. All made in a traditional farmhouse kitchen.

Blencathra Bakery
High Row Farm, Threlkeld, Keswick,
Cumbria CA12 4SF
017687 79256
Qualified baker/confectioner with over 30 years experience producing homemade cakes, tea breads, scones and hot puddings. No artificial colours or additives. Occasion cakes and delivery service available.

Brookside Products Ltd
Harbour View, Glasson Estate, Maryport CA15 8NT
01900815757
Producers of fine smoked Scottish salmon, using superior Atlantic salmon, which is authentically cold smoked over oak wood chips. Able to supply a wide range of salmon products.

Broughton Village Bakery
Prince's Street, Broughton in Furness,
Cumbria LA20 6HN
01229 716284
Handmade specialty breads such as tomato and basil, sunflower seed, mature cheddar, baked using organic stoneground flour milled in Cumbria. Selection of cakes, desserts and quiches. Specialist diets catered for. Café and B & B above the bakery.

Bryson's of Keswick
42 Main Street, Keswick, Cumbria CA12 5JD
017687 72257
j.buckley@btclick.com
Producers of a wide range of breads, cakes, morning goods and creams. Specialties include Lakeland plum bread, finest fruit cake, florentines and Borrowdale tea bread.

Burbush Penrith Ltd
The Eden Game Bakery, Gilwilly Road, Penrith,
Cumbria CA11 9BL
01768 863841
www.edengamebakery.co.uk
Range of hand-raised pies, paté, single pre-portioned meals, pasties, plus Cumberland sausage rolls.

Cartmel Village Shop
The Square, Cartmel, Grange over Sands, Cumbria
LA11 6QB
015395 36201
www.stickytoffeepudding.co.uk
Homemade sticky toffee pudding.

Coniston Lodge Private Hotel
Coniston, Cumbria LA21 8HH
015394 41201
www.coniston-lodge.com
Homemade produce: marmalade, jams, chutneys, Coniston Lodge's gingerbread, wheatmeal biscuits, fudge. Orders for luxury Christmas pudding taken.

Country Fare
Dale Foot Farm , Mallerstang, Kirkby Stephen,
Cumbria CA17 4JT
017683 71173
www.country-fare.co.uk
A range of home baked sticky toffee puddings, fruit cakes. Items made to order.

Country Flavour
15 High Street, Kirkby Stephen,
Cumbria CA17 4SG
017683 71124
chris@countryflavour.fsnet.co.uk
Homemade fudge, toffee, lemon cheese, herb jellies, preserves and rum butter.

Country Puddings
Lodge Farm, Dacre, Penrith, Cumbria CA11 0HH
017684 86675
www.countrypuddings.co.uk
Traditional homemade puddings. Sticky toffee, sticky ginger, chocolate fudge and luxury Christmas pudding.

D's Homemade Delights
High Mansriggs, Ulverston, Cumbria LA12 7PY
01229 582440
dshomemadedelights@hotmail.com
A range of homemade cakes and biscuits.

Hazelmere Café and Bakery
1-2 Yewbarrow Terrace, Grange over Sands, Cumbria LA11 6ED
015395 32972
Traditional bakers and confectioners using local and original recipes.

Jan's Confectionery Treats
19 High Greenbank, Ambleside, Cumbria LA22 9BE
015394 31608
Novelty Cumbrian confectionery products. Uniquely designed chocolates, fudge and biscuits.

Jean's Pantry
4 Scaur Terrace, Tebay, Penrith, Cumbria CA10 3TN
015396 24413
Chocolate cakes, apple pies, ginger biscuits, mince pies, almond tarts, blackcurrant pies, Viennese fingers.

Kennedy's Fine Chocolates Ltd
The Old School, Orton, Penrith, Cumbria CA10 3RU
015396 24781
www.kennedys-chocolates.co.uk
Manufacturers of fine handmade chocolates.

Le Pain de Paris
9/11 Mill Yard, Staveley, Near Kendal, Cumbria LA8 9LR
01539 822102
Producers of traditional bread, speciality and patisserie.

Moody Baker Co-op Ltd
3 West View, Front Street, Alston CA9 3SF
Bakery co-operative producing varied specialties. Natural and local ingredients used where possible. Extensive lunchtime selection, vegetarian snacks, Cumberland sausage pie, sausage rolls and fruit/nut/seed energy bars.

Oak Street Bakery
1 Oak Street, Windermere, Cumbria, LA23 1BH
015394 48284
Specialist bakers producing a quality range of continental breads, tray bakes and cakes. All made on the open plan premises.

Old Dairy Baking
Barkin House, Gatebeck, Kendal, Cumbria LA8 0HX
015395 67277
Homemade cakes, preserves and pickles. Baking for special occasions. Orders freshly made from the farm. Natural, locally sourced ingredients and Fair Trade products used wherever possible.

Old Smokehouse and Truffles and Chocolates
Brougham Hall, Brougham, Penrith, Cumbria CA10 2DE
01768 867772
www.the-old-smokehouse.co.uk
Renowned for fine smoked foods using high quality game, meat, fish and cheese. Also handmade truffles made from fine chocolate, fresh cream, fruit and alcohol.

Sarah Nelson's Grasmere Gingerbread Shop
Church Cottage, Grasmere, Ambleside, Cumbria LA22 9SW
015394 35428
www.grasmeregingerbread.co.uk
The only producers of Sarah Nelson's original celebrated Grasmere Gingerbread. Famous for its secret recipe and baked fresh every day since 1854. Mail order service available.

Saunders Fine Handmade Chocolates
Stocks Garth, Rosley, Wigton, Cumbria CA7 8BZ
016973 45597
bobcullen@btinternet.com
Chocolates made and sold at Rheged Visitors Centre. Natural ingredients and original recipes used, including peach 'n' saffron and banoffee cup. Chocolates can be seen being made by hand.

Staff of Life
Berry's Yard, Finkle Street, Kendal, Cumbria LA9 4AB
01539 741240
staffoflife@ukf.net
Handmade specialty breads from traditional and original recipes. Italian style savoury loaves with herbs, seeds and various fillings including pesto, pistachios and garlic with wild mushrooms. Organic wheat, rye and barley recipes, fruited teabreads, seasonal specials, and the Kendal Wygge. Bespoke breads to your own designs available. Shop.

Susan's Home Baking
3 Tarnside, Ulverston, Cumbria LA12 7EH
susanreidy@ukf.net
Novelty biscuits.

Ultimate Plum Pudding Company
9-10 Beezon Trading Estate, Kendal,
Cumbria LA9 6BW
01539 733329
sales@ultimateplumpudding.co.uk
Luxury Christmas puddings and brandy butter.

The Village Bakery Melmerby Ltd
Melmerby, Penrith, Cumbria CA10 1HE
01768 881515
www.village-bakery.com
Producers of good, healthy food, made from natural
ingredients, baked in an oven fired with wood grown
in a sustainable environment.

Wooden Spoon Fudge Company
1 Colton Cottages, Colton, Ulverston,
Cumbria LA12 8HF
01229 861029
waller@uk4free.net
Homemade fudge with no artificial additives,
preservatives or flavourings.

MEATS

Barwise Aberdeen Angus
Barwise Hall, Appleby, Cumbria CA16 6TD
017683 53430
barwise@btinternet.com
Aberdeen Angus beef from the pedigree herd and
lamb, traditionally grass reared to the highest
standard of traceability, health and welfare. On
farm maturation and preparation.

Border County Foods
The Old Vicarage, Crosby on Eden, Carlisle,
Cumbria CA6 4QZ
01228 573500
www.cumberland-sausage.net,
Best Black/Offal Pudding Award 2004 for
Savoury Dux. Free range meat, using pigs
similar to the old Cumberland which gave
Cumberland sausage its name.

Bromley Green Farm
Ormside, Appleby, Cumbria CA16 6EJ
017683 53327
bromleygreen@ukf.net
Home produced lamb and Aberdeen Angus beef.
Born and raised on an all-grass farm. Natural
maturation and Farm Assured.

Buckles Farm,
Barras, Kirkby Stephen, Cumbria CA17 4ES
017683 41917
krisb@totalise.co.uk
Producers of hill lamb and pigs for many years.
Regulars at the Carlisle and Kendal Cumbrian
farmers' markets. Extensive range of speciality
sausages, prize winning pork pies, dry-cured bacon
and ready meals.

Carrock Meats
Linewaith, Hesketh Newmarket, Wigton,
Cumbria CA7 8JT
017684 84272
Producers of a variety of specialised gluten-free,
high meat content Cumberland sausages, and
other gluten-free products. Suppliers of fresh
Lakeland lamb in half of whole lamb packs or cut
to order.

Country Cuts Organic Meats
Bridge End Farm, Santon Bridge, Holmrook,
Cumbria CA19 1UY
019467 26256
www.country-cuts.com
Home produced organically certified UK2 lamb,
beef and mutton, all vac packed. National delivery.
All meats are clover fed from meadow pastures.

Cranstons Ltd
Ullswater Road, Penrith, Cumbria CA11 7EH
01768 868680
cranstons@globalnet.co.uk
Cumberland sausages, pork pies and ready meals.

Croft Farm Meats
The Croft, Houghton, Carlisle, Cumbria CA3 0LD
01228 549628
susan@aglionby.demon.co.uk
Lamb and beef from the environmentally friendly
farm (in organic conversion). Available is Longhorn
beef and lamb, bred in Houghton. Some preserves
also made from homegrown fruit.

Cumbrian Fellbred Products Ltd
Crookland Road, Ackenthwaite, Milnthorpe,
Cumbria LA7 7LR
015395 63232,
Runner-up for the North West Producer of the
Year 2004. Winner of Best Beef and Sausage
with additives 2004. Traditionally reared
Cumbrian lamb and beef.

D and M Hughes
Silver Lea, Kirklinton, Carlisle, Cumbria CA6 6DG
01228 675546
hugh_ruth@yahoo.co.uk
High quality organic beef born and reared at Silver Lea. Supplied in a variety of packs suitable for freezing.

Farmersharp.co.uk
Diamond Buildings, Pennington Lane, Lindal in Furness, Cumbria LA12 0LA
01229 588299
www.farmersharp.co.uk
Best Air Dried Meat Award-winner 2004. Specialists in Herdwick lamb and lamb products, Galloway beef and beef products. Producers of Cumberland ham and bacon, Cumberland sausage and Herdwick lamb sausage. Mail order service across UK.

Furness Fish, Poultry and Game Supplies
Stockbridge Lane, Off Dalton Gate, Ulverston, Cumbria, LA12 7BG
01229 585037
www.morcambebayshrimps.co.uk
Best Savoury Pie/Pastry Award-winner 2004 for Quack Oink Pie. Morecambe Bay potted shrimps in butter, caught locally by fishermen. Boiled and cooked in butter with spices. All types of local game including a unique selection of game pies/smoked fish/meals.

Hallsford Butchery Ltd
Hallsford, Haggbeck, Hethersgill, Carlisle, Cumbria CA6 6JD
01228 577329
www.hallsford.co.uk
A family farm supplying quality lamb, and beef from their Shorthorn herd. Order via website.

Higginsons Butchers
Keswick House, Main Street, Grange over Sands, Cumbria LA11 6AB
015395 34367
Extensive range of fresh meat, pies, sausages, bacon and hams.

Ian Little
Helm Croft, Barrows Green, Kendal, Cumbria LA8 0AA
015395 60128
Beef.

Kendal Rough Fell Sheep Meat Producers
Hill Carlingill, Tebay, Penrith, Cumbria CA10 3XX
015396 24661
jhwilson@kencomp.net
Half and quarter packs of lamb from Kendal's local breed of sheep, kept traditionally.

Lune Valley Beef, Pork and Lamb
Nether Hall Farm, Mansergh, Kirkby Lonsdale, Cumbria LA6 2EW
015242 73193
www.rearednaturally.co.uk
Meat.

Mike Naylor
Middle Row, Wasdale Head, Seascale, Cumbria CA20 1EX
019467 26306
Home produced Herdwick lamb and mutton. Half and whole lambs for freezing. Mail order.

The Old Smokehouse
Brougham Hall, Brougham, Penrith, Cumbria CA10 2DE
01768 867772
www.the-old-smokehouse.co.uk
Renowned for fine smoked foods using high quality game, meat, fish and cheese. Also handmade truffles made from fine chocolate, fresh cream, fruit and alcohol.

Saddleback Foods
Scarfoot, Plumpton, Penrith CA11 9PF
017684 80100
www.saddlebackfoods.co.uk
Situated in Lakeland surroundings within the shadow of Blencathra (Saddleback). Producers of smoked and cured meats, game, poultry and fish. A range of cheeses, ready meals, patés and specialty sausages using locally sourced ingredients.

Savin Hill Farm
The Barn Owls, Savin Hill, Lyth Valley, Kendal, Cumbria LA8 8DJ
015395 68410
www.savin-hill.co.uk
Winner of Best Pork Award 2004.
Pure bred British White cattle and Middle White pigs, all registered pedigree stock. Quality producers of high class marbled beef, pork and dry-cured bacon and hams.

Shaws Farm Produce
13a Eden Street, Silloth, Cumbria CA7 4AD
016973 31181
www.shawmeats.co.uk
Producers of a wide range of sausages and bacon from Cumbrian pork. Bacon is cured the traditional way. Pies filled with local meat. Wild venison in stock.

Stainton Meats
Storth End Farm, Stainton, Kendal,
Cumbria LA8 0DZ
015395 60674
Locally produced, naturally reared pork and lamb.

Stevenson's Quality Farm Meats
Bow Top Farm, Hutton Roof, Penrith,
Cumbria CA11 0XS
01768 484237
Sausages produced for over 26 years. Home cured
ham, bacon and smoked sausages. A range of
local meats including poultry, some game, beef,
lamb and pork.

Stonyhead Hall Farm
Sunbiggin, Orton, Penrith, Cumbria CA10 3SQ
015396 24456
Pigs are farm reared in a stress free environment,
producing tender, succulent pork.

Whiteholme Farm Organic Meat
Whiteholme, Roweltown, Carlisle,
Cumbria CA6 6LJ
016977 48058
whiteholmefarm@hotmail.com
An organic livestock farm. Organic meat is
prepared at the farm butchery and sold direct to
local customers.

Windy Hill and Kitridding Farm
Lupton, Kirkby Lonsdale, Cumbria LA6 2QA
015395 67484
christine@kitridding.co.uk
Traditionally reared Swaledale lamb and home bred
beef and homemade sausages.

CURED MEATS

Richard Woodall Ltd
Lane End, Waberthwaite, Millom,
Cumbria LA19 5YJ
01229 717237
www.richardwoodall.co.uk
Producers of traditional dry-cured hams, bacons,
sausage and Cumbria air dried hams using farm
reared pork. Traditional recipes and techniques used.

Slack's Limited
Newlands Farm, Raisbeck, Orton, Penrith,
Cumbria CA10 3SG
015396 24667
slacks@fsbdial.co.uk
Producers of home cured bacon and gammon, air
dried and matured, green and smoked. A range of
traditional sausages and specialty cooked hams, plus
bacon, sausage and cooked ham produced from
free range, antibiotic and growth promoter free pork.

Steadmans
2 Finkle Street, Sedbergh, Cumbria LA10 5BZ
015396 20431, 015396 21719
www.steadmans-butchers.co.uk
Locally produced meats, dry-cured bacons and
hams, and homemade meat products.

SEAFOOD

Bessy Beck Trout Farm
Newbiggin on Lune, Kirkby Stephen,
Cumbria CA17 4LY
015396 23303
Three fishing lakes and a farm shop, selling freshly
caught trout, smoked trout paté, trout fillets, smoked
and vacuum packed on the premises. Postal service
available. Float rod hire.

Brookside Products
Harbour View, Glasson Estate, Maryport,
Cumbria CA15 8NT
01900 815757
brkside@globalnet.co.uk
Producers of Scottish smoked salmon.

Cumberland Cold Storage
Whitehaven, Cumbria
01900 819 700
Winner of Best Fish Award 2004. Mackerel
graded and filleted on site, brined traditionally
and hot smoked.

Hawkshead Trout Farm
The Boat House, Ridding Wood, Hawkshead,
Ambleside LA22 0QF
015394 36541
www.hawkshead.demon.co.uk,
Specialising in organic fish for the retail trade,
caterers and mail order. Farm shop, also available
at farmers' markets and trade shows.

BEVERAGES

Barratt and Keegan
Cowmire Hall, Crosthwaite, Kendal,
Cumbria LA8 8JJ
015395 68200
cowmirehall@ecosse.net
Damsons from the Lyth Valley and surrounding
area. Married to London Gin, can be served as an
aperitif and a liqueur.

Dent Brewery
Hollins, Cowgill, Dent, Sedbergh,
Cumbria LA10 5GH
015396 25326
martin@dentbrewery.co.uk
A small craft brewery. They use their own spring
water to produce award-winning beers.

Hawkshead Brewery
Town End, Hawkshead, Cumbria LA22 0JU
015394 36111
Producer of Hawkshead Bitter, Hawkshead Best.
Bottled beers are Hawkshead Gold and Red, both
available in Booths.

Lakeland Soft Drinks Ltd
1 Redlonning Industrial Estate, Hensingham,
Whitehaven CA28 6SJ
01946 690777
Lakeland spring waters; still, sparkling and
flavoured.

Lakeland Willow Water
Cartmel Valley Springs Ltd, Willow House, Moor
Lane, Flookburgh, Cumbria LA11 7LS
015395 59452
www.lakelandwillowwater.com
Unique spring water containing natural salicin.

Strawberry Bank Liqueurs
Wood Yeat Barn, Crosthwaite, Kendal,
Cumbria LA8 8HX
015395 68812
damsongin@aol.com
Producers of damson beer and damson gin from
the fruit grown in their own orchard and those of
other local growers in the Lyth Valley. Other fruit
liqueurs from pure fruit juices also available.

Think Drink
Clarks Cottage, Dent Sedbergh,
Cumbria LA10 5QT
015396 25504
john.sheard@ntlworld.com
A small apple juice producing business. Apples
sourced mainly from Cumbrian orchards containing
many ancient Cumbrian varieties, providing a
range of distinctive flavours.

SPECIALTY FOODS

Demels
Cross Lane, Ulverston, Cumbria LA12 9DQ
01229 580580
www.demels.co.uk
Chutneys from original Sri Lankan family recipes.

J and J Graham
Market Square, Penrith, Cumbria CA11 7BS
01768 862281
Fine food hall specialising in local produce.

Made in Cumbria Trading Ltd
County Offices, Busher Walk, Kendal,
Cumbria LA9 4RQ
01539 732736
Retailers of various specialty food products such as
potted char, rum nicky and chocolate caramel slice.
Operates the Food from the Fells retail outlets.

Natural Health Company
11 Riverbank Road, Kendal LA9 5JS
01539 735 004
Producers of organic vegetarian pasties.

Perogies by Suzan
Lock Bank Farm, Sedbergh, Cumbria LA10 5HE
015396 20252
lockbank@uk4free.net
Perogies are a homemade traditional Ukranian
food. Handmade, they consist of wholesome
ingredients; dough folded around a variety of
fillings. Suitable for vegetarians.

PRESERVES

Claire's Handmade
Newlands House, Mealsgate, Wigton,
Cumbria CA7 1AB
016973 71567
Producer of homemade preserves, ketchups, pickles
and chutneys.

Country Conserves
128 Main Street, St Bees, Cumbria CA27 0DE
01946 822710
Seasonal jams, marmalades, chutneys and pickles.
Unusual recipes. Homemade with no artificial
preservatives, colouring or flavouring.

Cumberland Mustard
16 Hill House Lane, Alston, Cumbria CA9 3TN
01434 381135
Fine regional honey mustards.

Hawkshead Relish Company
The Square, Hawkshead, Cumbria LA22 0NZ
015394 36614
www.hawksheadrelish.co.uk
Developed on the back of the Hawkshead Whigs
Café/Bistro. A family run business with a range of
quality hand prepared relishes, mustards and
sauces.

Hutton Roof Hall
Hutton Roof, Kirkby Lonsdale, Cumbria
015242 71435
North West Producer of the Year 2004 and
Winner of Best Preserve / Pickle 2004.
Homemade, handmade jams and marmalades,
using village supplies of fruit and ingredients
from Booths. Available at local farm shops and
markets.

Richardsons Tearooms
151 Queen Street, Whitehaven,
Cumbria CA28 7BA
01946 599860
tearooms@aol.com
Homemade jams, preserves and rum butter
traditionally made with fresh, local ingredients.

SC Farming
Moss Howe Farm, Witherslack,
Grange over Sands LA11 6SA
015395 52585
s.c.farming@mosshowe.fsnet.co.uk
Jams, chutneys, fruits in alcohol and fruit coulis
made from fruits in season grown on the estate.
Venison culled from the estate herd.

Wild and Fruitful
Hillside, Cuddy Lonning, Wigton CA7 0AA
016973 44304
clover@maryport1.fsnet.co.uk
www.wildandfruitful.co.uk
Producers of unique batches of handmade jams,
jellies, chutneys, oils, vinegars and salts using local,
hand picked, unsprayed ingredients where possible.
Unusual combinations and old favourites. Jars
labelled with the origin of ingredients and
alternative uses.

SPICES AND HERBS

Isaac Armstrong and Sons
Sandgate House, Sandgate, Penrith,
Cumbria CA11 7TJ
01768 862394
A wide selection of herbs, vegetables, shrubs and
trees, basket plants and sweet peas, all grown in
the nursery.

Red Dial Nurseries
Damson Cottage, Catterlen, Penrith,
Cumbria CA11 0BQ
01768 895718
the_dial@ukf.net
Specialising in unusual, rare plants as well as some
basic lines, including herbs. Many grown from
seeds collected on annual collecting expeditions,
particularly to the Himalayas. Plants grown from
cuttings received from private collectors.

SOUP

Jeremy's Soups Ltd
The Old Canteen, Unit 4, Appleby Business Park,
Drawbriggs Lane, Appleby,
Westmorland CA16 6HX
017683 53311
helen.kent@ukonline.co.uk
Producers of a range of freshly made, traditionally
flavoured cream and non cream soups. Available in
600g tubs and 5 litre catering buckets.

FLOUR

Carrs Flour Mills Ltd
Old Croft, Stanwix, Carlisle, Cumbria CA3 9BA
01228 554600
www.carrs-flourmills.co.uk
Producers of quality flours since 1836, they are first
choice for many of the UK's leading craft bakers. A
comprehensive range of retail flour, Delia's favourite
Breadmaker Blends and Makefresh, an exciting new-
to-retail mix for making fresh yoghurt at home.

Little Salkeld Watermill
Little Salkeld, Penrith, Cumbria CA10 1NN
01768 881523
www.organicmill.co.uk
Winner of Best Bakery Product Award 2004
with Granarius Bread. Organic and biodynamic
flours.

FARM SHOPS

Greystone Farm Shop and Tearoom
Greystone House, Stainton, Penrith,
Cumbria CA11 0EF
01768 864 443

Howbarrow Organic Farm
Cartmel, Grange over Sands, Cumbria LA11 7SS
015395 36330
www.howbarroworganic@demon.co.uk
Producers of pork, lamb, bacon, sausage, poultry
and eggs, as well as a large number of in season
vegetables, herbal tinctures, herbs and flowers.
Open farm policy, encouraging visitors to see an
alternative way of farming.

Low Sizergh Barn
Low Sizergh Farm, Sizergh, Kendal,
Cumbria LA8 8AE
015395 60426
Farm shop and tearoom with speciality regional
foods.

Plumgarths Farm Shop
Crook Road, Kendal, Cumbria LA8 8LX
01539 736136
www.plumgarths.co.uk
Local meats, pies, cakes and meat hampers.

Pow Heads Meat Farm
Pow Heads, Sandale, Mealsgate, Wigton,
Cumbria CA7 1DF
016973 71325
maries@globalnet.co.uk,
A small family farm producing meat with traditional
flavour. Animals matured slowly, free range where
possible. Rare and commercial breeds. Beef, lamb,
pork, traditional Cumberland sausages, duck,
chicken, Christmas geese and turkeys. Home cured
ham and bacon.

Sillfield Farm Products
Sillfield Farm, Endmoor, Kendal, Cumbria LA8 0HZ
015395 67609
enquiries@sillfield.co.uk
Farm made products mostly from revived recipes of
the area. Westmorland cheese, Mallerstang ewe
cheese, Cumberland sausage, rare breeds, pork,
own range of wild boar products. Hand-raised pies
and dry-cured bacon available.

FARMERS' MARKETS

Brampton Farmers' Market
Moot Hall, Brampton, Cumbria
01539 732 736
www.madeincumbria.co.uk
The characteristic Moot Hall provides the backdrop
to this small, varied farmers' market. The last
Saturday of every month.

Brough Farmers' Market
Memorial Hall, Brough, Kirkby Stephen, Brough,
Cumbria CA17 4AS
01768342135
brough.farmersmarket@virgin.net
Set at the foot of the Pennines in an historic
coaching village, wide range of local produce.
Third Saturday of each month.

Carlisle Farmers' Market
City Centre, Carlisle, Cumbria CA3 8QG
01539 732 736
www.madeincumbria.co.uk
In the heart of Carlisle, the market offers a great
selection of locally produced food. The first Friday
of the month.

Egremont Farmers' Market
Market Hall, Market Street, Egremont
01539 732 734
www.madeincumbria.co.uk
Nestling at the foot of Ennerdale fells. The third
Friday of each month.

Kendal Farmers' Market
Market Place, Kendal, Cumbria
01539 732 734
www.madeincumbria.co.uk
Spacious venue provides an opportunity to produce
a range of local produce. The last Friday of every
month.

Orton Farmers' Market
Orton Market Hall, J38 off the M6
Held on the second Saturday monthly.

Penrith Farmers' Market
Town Centre, Penrith, Cumbria CA11 7BY
anne.meston@eden.gov.uk
Held in the historic setting of the Market Square,
selling a range of local produce. The third Tuesday
of every month.

Ulverston Farmers' Market
Market Hall, Ulverston, Cumbria LA12 7LR
01539 732 734
www.madeincumbria.co.uk
In the traditional lakeland town, offering a selection
of local produce. Takes place on the third Saturday
of each month.

Whitehaven Farmers' Market
Safeway Car Park, Whitehaven, Cumbria
01539 732 734
www.madeincumbria.co.uk
This historic harbour town provides a great setting
for this farmers' market, held on the first Saturday
of the month.

EATING PLACES

The Drunken Duck
Barngates, Ambleside, Lake District,
Cumbria LA22 0NG
01539 36347
www.drunkenduckinn.co.uk
Pub and restaurant using local produce.

L'Enclume
Cartmel Village, near Grange over Sands,
Cumbria LA11 6PZ
015395 36362
www.lenclume.co.uk
Gastronomic restaurant, home to Simon Rogan's
cuisine.

Holker Food
Cark-in-Cartmell, Grange over Sands LA11 7PL
015395 59084 www.holker-hall.co.uk
Tourist outlet and food hall.

Lucy's of Ambleside and Lucy's on a Plate
Church Street, Ambleside, Cumbria LA22 0BU
015394 32288
www.lucysofambleside.co.uk
Specialist grocers and café restaurants with
regional produce.

The Punch Bowl Inn
Crosthwaite, near Kendal, Cumbria LA8 8HR
015395 68237
Restaurant under management of regional chef
Steven Doherty.

The Queens Head Inn
Tirril, near Penrith, Cumbria CA10 2JF
01768 863219
www.queensheadinn.co.uk
Gastropub serving local produce.

Regent Hotel
Waterhead Bay, Ambleside, Cumbria CA22 0ES
015394 32254
www.regentlakes.co.uk

The Royal Oak
Bongate, Appleby in Westmorland,
Cumbria CA16 6UN
Part of Mortal Man Inns chain. Restaurant serving
fresh dishes using local produce.

The Snooty Fox
Main Street, Kirkby Lonsdale, Cumbria LA6 2AH
015242 71308
Part of Mortal Man inns chain. Imaginative dishes
using local ingredients.

TASTE Food Bar
Rheged – The Village in the Hill, Redhills, Penrith,
Cumbria CA11 0DQ
01768 868 000
www.rheged.com
British food and drink. Also a Made in Cumbria
shop.

Whitewater Hotel
The Lakeland Village, Newby Bridge,
Cumbria LA12 8PX
015395 31133
www.whitewater-hotel.co.uk
Riverside restaurant serving local produce.

CATERING COMPANIES

Andrew Southcott Catering
Unit 6, Airfield Approach Business Park,
Flookburgh, Grange over Sands LA11 7LS
015395 59090
www.southcottcatering.co.uk
Outside catering company specialising in weddings,
corporate hospitality and outside events, from Royal
occasions to product launches.

LANCASHIRE

Made in Lancashire
Contact: Harriet Clayton
Rural Business Centre, Myerscough
College, Bilsbarrow, Preston PR3 0RY
01995 64255
harriet@madeinlancs.co.uk
www.madeinlancs.co.uk

DAIRY AND EGGS

AD and PE Shorrock
New House Farm, Ford Lane, Goosnargh,
Preston PR3 2FJ
01772 865250
Cheese making has been a tradition for three
generations of the Shorrock family and the same
recipes are still used.

Alston Dairy Ltd
Alston Lane, Longridge, Preston,
Lancashire PR3 3BN
01772 782621
www.alstondairy.co.uk
Traditional farmhouse handmade yoghurts. Fresh
from the family farm.

Brades Farm Dairy
Farleton, Lancaster, Lancashire LA2 9LF
015242 21589
Quality milk and cream from own dairy herd.

Butlers Farmhouse Cheeses
Wilson Fields Farm, Inglewhite, Preston PR3 2LH
01995 640827
www.butlerscheeses.co.uk
Producer of traditional, handmade farmhouse
cheese using old family recipes and local
Lancashire milk.

Carron Lodge Ltd
Park Head Farm, Inglewhite, Preston PR3 2LN
01995 640352
carronlodge@talk21.com
Producers of award-winning farmhouse cheese from their pedigree herd of cows. Also importers, wholesalers and distributors of cheese.

Cliftons Farm
Inglewhite, Preston PR3 2LP
01995 640 564
Dairy producer of milk, cream and ice cream.

Cringlebrook Farm
Ashley Lane, Goosnargh, Preston PR3 2EE
01772 865 279
Producers of cheese using own goat milk.

Dew-Lay
Garstang, Preston, Lancashire PR3 0PR
01995 602335
www.dewlay.com
Territorial and regional cheeses. Grated, sliced and prepacked available.

Dowson Dairies Ltd
Hawkshaw Farm, Longsight Road,
Clayton le Dale, Blackburn BB2 7JA
01254 812407
eb.dowson@virgin.net
Producers of a range of dairy products. Suppliers to milkmen, hotels, restaurants and the wholesale/retail trade.

Holwood Cheese
Hallidays Farm and Dairy, Bilsborrow, Preston,
Lancashire PR3 0RU
01995 640325
info@mrsdowsons.co.uk
Relatively small producers of quality handmade cheeses carried out on their own farm, producing territorial cheeses using milk from Farm Assured pedigree Holsteins.

JJ Sandham Ltd
Rostock Dairy, Garstang Road, Barton,
Preston PR3 5AA
01995 640247
jjsandham@aol.com
Manufacturers of award-winning Lancashire cheese since 1929.

Leagram Farm Dairy
Nature Haven, New House Barn, Goose Lane,
Chipping PR3 2QB
01995 61442
Organic cheeses including traditional territorials and additive cheeses.

Little Town Larder
Chipping Lane, Thornley, Preston,
Lancashire PR3 2TB
01772 782429
sales@littletown.prestel.co.uk
Quality yoghurts, probiotic drinks, crème fraiche and soured cream.

Lower Barker Farm
Inglewhite, Preston, Lancashire PR3 2LH
01995 640334
lowbark@btinternet.com
Producers and suppliers of milk using fresh milk from own farm herd.

Mrs Kirkham's Lancashire Cheese
Beesley Farm, Mill Lane, Goosnargh, Preston,
Lancashire PR3 2FL
01772 865335
Traditional farmhouse Lancashire cheeses.

Singleton's Dairy Ltd
Mill Farm, Preston Road, Longridge,
Preston PR3 3AN
01772 782112
www.singletons.uk.com
Dairy (Processed). Singleton's cheeses began in a farmhouse kitchen. 20 years later a brand new dairy room full of trophies for product excellence was built.

Slaters Ices
Ice Works, Cross Street, nelson BB9 7NQ
01282 614 950
Parlour selling dairy ice cream, fudge and patisseries.

Top Oth Meadow Farm Eggs
Top Oth Meadow Farm, Meadow Head Lane,
Norden, Rochdale OL11 5UL
01706 658 771
Free range egg producer.

FRUIT AND VEGETABLES

Birchwood Nurseries
Cropper Road, Blackpool, Lancashire FY4 5LB
01253 699948
margaret@atkinson131.freeserve.co.uk
A small family concern growing pesticide-free tomatoes.

Growing with Grace Ltd
Clapham Nursery, Clapham, Lancaster LA2 8ER
015242 51723
www.growingwithgrace.co.uk
Organic produce.

Growing with Nature
Bradshaw Lane Nursery, Pilling, Preston PR3 6AX
01253 790046
Fruit and veg.

Jigsaw Environmental
Main Street, Gisburn, Clitheroe BB7 6HN
01200 415979
Growers of organic fruit, vegetables, salads and cut flowers.

RA Owen and Sons
Brookfield Farm, Hall Lane, Simonswood,
Lancashire L33 4XX
0151 548 4611
julie@ra.owen-freeserve.co.uk

Sharrock's Fresh Produce
Chain Caul Way, Riversway, Preston PR2 2YL
01772 724 444

Sykes Fold Farm
Burned House Lane, Presall, Poulton le Fylde,
Lancashire FY6 0PQ
01253 790712
Wide range of fresh homegrown vegetables.

W and EF Neale
The Farm, Martin Lane, Burscough,
Ormskirk L40 0RT
01704 892247
freda.neale@ic24.net
Winners of Best Fruit and Veg Award 2004
with Ambo Potato. The Neale family produce
traditionally grown vegetables, free range eggs
and lemon curd, jams, pickles and chutneys.

Wareings
Johnsons Farm, Johnsons Meanygate, Tarleton,
Preston PR4 6LQ
01772 815629
wareings4veg@btopenworld
A family run business growing seasonal vegetables
and salads with bedding plants in the spring.
Selling at local farmers' markets.

BAKERY AND CONFECTIONERY

Ant-Ems Bakery
1 Burnley Road East, Waterfoot, Rossendale,
Lancashire BB4 9AG
01706 216393
All produce is handmade in the bakery. A varied
range to offer, pheasant, apricot and chestnut pie.

Bashall Barn
Bashall Eaves, Clitheroe,
Lancashire BB7 3LQ
01200 428964
simon-barnes@btconnect.com
Country food and gift shop with café and new
function room.

Cottage Cookies
17 Brunswick Street, Darwen, Lancashire BB3 2AJ
01254 762178
A small biscuit manufacturing business. Traditional,
homemade recipes, sweet and sugar free cookies.

Farm Shop Alston
Manor House Farm, Alston, Longridge,
Preston PR3 3BQ
01772 784 169
Homemade cakes, biscuits and pies.

Farmhouse Biscuits Limited
Brook Street, Nelson, Lancashire BB9 9PX
01282 613520
www.farmhouse-biscuits.co.uk
Traditional handbaked biscuits.

Farmhouse Fare Ltd
Anderson House, Lincoln Way, Salthill,
Clitheroe BB7 1QL
01200 453110
www.farmhousefare.co.uk
All puddings are made using natural ingredients
with no additives or preservatives.

The Ingleton Gingerbread Company
Oakroyd Bakery, 17 Station Road, High Bentham,
Lancaster LA2 7LH
015242 63353
www.oakroyd.co.uk
Handmade quality puddings and cakes made to
traditional recipes.

The Little Farmhouse Bakery
Cunliffe Fold Farm, Blackleach Lane, Salwick,
Preston PR4 0RY
01772 690622
A small bakery and farm shop selling traditionally
baked bread, cakes and savouries.

Park Farm
Walmersley, Bury BL9 5NP
01706 823 577
Farm shop and tearoom selling home baked pies,
cakes and biscuits.

Philippa's Fine Foods
9 Chaucer Close, Eccleston, Chorley, Preston,
Lancashire PR7 5UJ
01257 450011
www.philippas.co.uk
Producer of a wide range of bakery products using
local and free range ingredients where possible.

Susan's Farmhouse Fudge
Gregson's Farm, Samlesbury, Preston,
Lancashire PR5 0UH
01772 877468
Homemade fudge, toffee and truffles.

Towers Pies
4 Newmarket Street, Bare, Morecambe,
Lancashire LA4 6BJ
01524 411611
Bakery producing a range of traditional pies.

MEATS

Alpes the Butchers Ltd
14 Shawbridge Street, Clitheroe,
Lancashire BB7 1LZ
01200 424519
Member of Q Guild of Butchers.

Bedfords of Blackburn Ltd
Cunliffe Road, Whitebirk Industrial Estate,
Blackburn BB1 5SU
01254 55483
www.bedfords-foodservice.co.uk
Established in the meat trade for over 60 years and
continues as a family business.

Bowland Forest Foods
Home Farm Office, Abbeystead, Lancaster,
Lancashire LA2 9BQ
01524 793558
www.bowlandforest.co.uk
Co-operative of accredited beef, lamb and pork
farms.

Bowland Outdoor Reared Pork
Bradshaw Barn, Craggs Farm, Lowgill,
Tatham LA2 8RB
015242 63031
Award-winner of Best Overall Sausage and
Pure Pork Sausage 2004. Home produced
fresh pork and pork products from the Forest
of Bowland.

Capra Products
7 King Street, Longridge, Preston,
Lancashire PR3 3RQ
01772 784881
A small producer of quality goat products, meat
and cheese.

Cockers Farm Shop
Limbrick, Chorley PR6 7EE
01257 268 743
Fresh meat from the farm, jams, preserves and
oven-ready meals.

DC Scott and Sons (Ormskirk) Ltd
25-27 Church Street, Ormskirk,
Lancashire L39 3AG
01695 572104
Butchers selling fine meat and meat products.

The Ellel Free Range Poultry Company
The Stables, Ellel Grange, Bay Horse,
Lancaster LA2 0HN
01524 751 200
info@ellelfreerangepoultry.co.uk
Free range poultry including chicken, guinea fowl,
Bronze turkeys and geese.

Farmhouse Direct
Long Ghyll Farms, Brock Close, Bleasdale Lane,
Bleasdale PR3 1UZ
01995 61799
www.farmhousedirect.com
A family run business selling high quality meats
direct from the farm. Highland beef, wild venison,
Gloucester Old Spot pork and dry-cured bacon.

Fayre Game
Lodge Lane Nurseries, Lodge Lane, Lytham FY8 5RP
01253 738 989
Quail farmers and game processors.

Gracemire Lamb
Gracemire Farm, Salwick, Preston,
Lancashire PR4 0SA
01772 690377
gracemire@netscapeonline.co.uk
Farm produced lamb to order.

Great House Farm
Helmshore, Rossendale, Lancashire BB4 4AJ
01706 212296
A family run farm consisting of 420 acres running a
flock of 720 sheep and 80 cows.

Hartley's Farm Foods
Nelson, Lancashire
01282 691 700
Winner of Best Cooked Meat Counter Product
2004 for Home Cooked Ham. Fine hams
available in various outlets.

Healthy Bite Farm Products
Hillthrope Farm, Knoll Lane, Little Hoole,
Preston PR4 4TB
01772 616565
A farming family firm producing sausages and
burgers from regional ingredients whenever possible.

Honeywell Meats
Eaves Lane, Woodplumpton, Preston,
Lancashire PR4 0BH
01772 690271
Butchers selling traditionally reared local meats.

Joe's Sausages
15 Greenhey's Place, East Gillibrands,
Skelmersdale WN8 9SA
01695 555506
www.joessausages.co.uk
Virtually fat free sausages, burgers and minces.

John Hargreaves Butchers
12a Preston New Road, Blackburn BB2 1AW
01254 52106
Local beef, lamb, pork, chicken, eggs, cooked meats
and cheeses, homemade sausages, preserves and
prepared meals.

Margerison's
Grange Farm, Parsonage Road, Wilpshire,
Blackburn, Lancashire BB1 4AG
078668 10242
johnandpearl@margerisongrange.freeserve.co.uk
Turkeys, chickens, sausages and burgers.

Mansergh Hall Lamb
Mansergh Hall, Kirkby Lonsdale, Via Carnforth,
Lancashire LA6 2EN
015242 71397
info@manserghhall.co.uk
RSPCA Freedom Foods lamb and rare breed pork
products.

PD Willacy
Springfield Farm, Berry's Lane, Poulton le Fylde,
Preston FY6 7LT
01253 883470
Free range chickens and eggs and barn reared
turkeys available as a whole bird or portions.

Pickups Butchers Ltd
Stall 4, Blackburn Market, Ainsworth Street,
Blackburn BB1 6AF
01254 57225
keith.pickup@ntlworld.com
British beef, lamb and pork.

RS Ireland The Black Pudding Company
Pudsville 2, Glentop Works, Stacksteds,
Bacup OL13 0NH
01706 872172
www.rsireland.co.uk
A range of handmade black puddings, using the
original recipe dating back to 1879.

Spout House Farm
Higher Wheelton, near Chorley,
Lancashire PR6 8HS
01254 830352
spouthousefarm@amserve.com
Quality home bred beef and lamb.

Swainson House Farm
Goosnargh Lane, Goosnargh, Preston,
Lancashire PR3 2JU
01772 865251
johnson.swarbrick@ic24.net
Goosnargh duckling, corn fed chickens, turkeys,
smoked duckling and chicken.

Udale Speciality Foods
Schola Green Lane, Morecambe,
Lancashire LA4 5QT
01524 411611, 01524 411677
www.udale.co.uk
Cumberland sausage, fresh meats, poultry and
game.

Weatheroak Ostrich Farm
Back Lane, Weeton, Preston,
Lancashire PR4 3HS
01253 836386
weather.oak@tiscali.co.uk
Winner of Best Poultry Award 2004 for Ostrich
Fillet. Ostrich is the healthy alternative to red
meat, low in fat, calories and cholesterol, high
in protein and iron.

CURED MEATS

Farmhouse Direct
Long Ghyll Farms, Brock Close, Bleasdale Lane,
Bleasdale PR3 1UZ
01995 61799
www.farmhousedirect.com
A small family run business, selling high quality
meats direct from the farm, including Highland
beef, wild venison, Gloucester Old Spot pork and
dry-cured bacon.

Mark Anthony Patés
162 Dock Street, Fleetwood, Lancashire FY7 6SB
01253 773073
Handmade patés and terrines supplied to the hotel
and catering industry.

Oakdene Farm Shop
Fleetwood Road, Greenhalgh, Kirkham PR4 3HE
01772 685882
Producers of dry cure bacon, gammon, burgers and various sausages.

SEAFOOD

High Seas Seafoods
Unit 30, Holme Mills Industrial Estate, Holme, Via Carnforth, Lancashire LA6 1RD
01524 781014
paulbarrah@kencomp.net
Manufacturer of creative seafood range of products, marinated in a range of home prepared spices and herbs. Cod, salmon, tuna, bass and whitefish. Products prepared and packed on site, delivered in refrigerated vehicles throughout the North West.

Lakeland Seafoods
Dockside, Dock Street, Fleetwood FY7 6NU
01253 772 656
Fresh and frozen seafoods.

BEVERAGES

Church Inn
Running Hill Gate, Uppermill,
near Oldham OL3 6LW
01457 820 902

Exchange Coffee Company
24 Wellgate, Clitheroe BB7 2DP
01200 442270
www.exchangecoffee.co.uk
Coffee roasted daily, over 50 coffees and 60 teas available in Victorian coffee houses.

Hart Brewery Ltd
Cartford Hotel, Cartford Lane, Little Eccleston, Preston PR3 0YP
01995 671686
Selection of beers available in about a hundred outlets, mostly in the North West. Pub onsite. Winner of Beer of the Festival at Southport's Sandgrounder Festival 2003.

Mawson's Traditional Drinks Ltd
Unit 11a, Newline Industrial Estate,
Bacup OL13 9RW1
01706 874 448
www.sarsaparilla.co.uk
Manufacturer and wholesaler of the Sarsaparilla and Dandelion and Burdock cordial. Available in various outlets.

Moorhouses Brewery Ltd
The Brewery, Moorhouses Street, Burnley, Lancashire BB11 5EN
01282 422864
info@moorhouses.co.uk
Winner of Best Alcoholic Drink Award 2004 with Pendle Witch Beer. Premier Bitter, Black Cat and Pride of Pendle also.

Phoenix Brewery
Green Lane, Heywood OL10 2EP
01706 627009
Successful micro brewery.

Roberts and Co
The Coffee Roastery, Art@Cedar Farm, Back Lane, Mawdesley, Ormskirk L40 3SY
01704 822433
Speciality fresh roasted coffees and teas.

SPECIALITY FOODS

Chilli Lime Deli
6 Bryers Croft, Wilpshire, Blackburn, Lancashire BB1 9JE
01254 247600
Quality deli stocking regional products.

City Deli
8b Winckley Street, Preston, Lancashire PR1 2AA
01772 204777
www.thecitydeli.com
Quality deli stocking regional products.

Country Harvest
Ingleton, Carnforth, Lancashire LA6 3PE
015242 42223
www.country-harvest.co.uk
Independent retailer with quality deli and meat counters.

PRESERVES

Hawkins Foods 2000 Ltd
Unit 7, Moorings Close Industrial Estate, Off Lower Hollinbank Street, Blackburn BB2 4AH
01772 794815
A pickle and chutney manufacturer specialising in handmade products from the South Asian region, aiming to bring to market products that are not currently available in the UK.

Holly Cottage Preserves
18 Slaidburn Avenue, Rawtenstall, Rossendale, Lancashire BB4 8JS
01706 260 666
Producer of an unusual range of preserves, jams, chutneys and pickles.

Honeycomb Co Ltd
Pennine Bee Farm, Stoney Lane, Ellel,
Lancaster LA2 0QY
01524 751347
www.honeycombcompany.co.uk
Quality honey products and preserves.

J and J Produce
Langdale House, Beech Road, Elswick,
Preston PR4 3YB
01995 670064
jeankathleen@hotmail.com
Homemade jams and preserves sold at local
farmers' markets.

SPICES AND HERBS

Bowlander Ltd
Mill House, Long Buildings, Sawley, Clitheroe,
Lancashire BB7 4LE
01200 449833
www.bowlander.co.uk
Spices and natural flavour ingredients.

Culinary Herbs
Rawcliffe Lodge, Bodkin Lane, Out Rawcliffe,
Preston PR3 6TL
01253 700311
helly.hall@virgin.net
Specialising in the local production and sale of the
more unusual herbs used in cookery, from angelica
to zrul.

McKinsey Healthy Herbs
Orrell Road, Orrell, Wigan, Lancashire WN5 8QZ
01695 632825
mckinsey_herbs@beeb.net
Family run organic herb nursery and tearoom
stocking over 150 varieties of herbs. Staff are
always available for advice.

PREPARED FOODS

Laila's Fine Foods
Unit 4-5 Lindun Industrial Park, Boundary Road,
Lytham St Annes FY8 5HU
01253 732 121
Eastern and western ready meals.

Mortimers Farmhouse Meals
Earnshaw Shire Farm, Ulnes Walton Lane, Ulnes
Walton, Leyland PR26 8LT
01772 423902
A range of traditional and modern meals all
entirely handmade with local farm vegetables, and
British beef.

SMOKED PRODUCE

Port of Lancaster Smokehouse
West Quay, Glasson Dock, Lancaster,
Lancashire LA2 0DB
01524 751493
www.glassonsmokehouse.co.uk
Traditionally smoked and gourmet foods along with
an extensive range of cheeses, preserves and
English fruit wines.

FARM SHOPS

Cockers Farm Shop
Limbrick, Chorley PR6 7EE
01257 268 743
Fresh meat from the farm, jams and preserves and
oven-ready meals.

Conder Green Farm Shop
Conder Green Farm, Conder Green, Lancaster,
Lancashire LA2 0AN
01524 752174
www.condergreenfarm.co.uk
Farm reared beef, lamb and pork.

Fairfield Farm Shop
Fairfield Farm, Longsight Road, Clayton le Dale,
Blackburn BB2 7JA
01254 812550
www.fairfieldfarm.co.uk
A pig farm producing home cured ham and bacon,
homemade sausages, local chicken and beef.

Farm Shop Alston
Manor House Farm, Alston, Longridge,
Preston PR3 3BQ
01772 784 169
Homemade cakes, biscuits and pies.

Huntley's of Samlesbury Limited
Huntleys Gate Farm, Whalley Road, Samlesbury,
Preston PR5 0UN
01772 877123
huntleys@samlesbury123.fsnet.co.uk
Manufacturers of quality ice cream and also sell
fresh fruit and vegetables, cheeses, jams and
preserves and home-reared meats.

Jigsaw Pantry
Fairfield House, Fairfield Street, Accrington,
Lancashire BB5 0LD
01254 381317
Jigsaw Pantry trains and employs disabled people
through their bakery and soon there will be a
delicatessen which will operate as a social
enterprise.

Mansergh Hall Farm Shop

Mansergh Hall, Kirkby Lonsdale, via Carnforth,
Lancashire LA6 2EN
015242 71397
www.manserghhall.co.uk
Nationally renowned for their own RSPA Freedom
Food Accredited Mansergh Hall lamb, produced
without the use of herbicides or pesticides.
Gloucester Old Spot pork, used for dry-cured
bacon. A wide variety of handmade sausages.

Oakdene Farm Shop

Fleetwood Road, Greenhalgh, Kirkham PR4 3HE
01772 685882
Producers of dry cure bacon, gammon, burgers and
various sausages.

Park Farm

Walmersley, Bury BL9 5NP
01706 823 577
Farm shop and tearoom selling home baked pies,
cakes and biscuits.

Slaters Ices

Ice Works, Cross Street, Nelson BB9 7NQ
01282 614 950
Parlour selling dairy ice cream, fudge and
patisseries.

W and EF Neale

The Farm, Martin Lane, Burscough,
Ormskirk L40 0RT
01704 892247
freda.neale@ic24.net
Winners of Best Fruit and Veg Award 2004
with Ambo Potato. The Neale family produce
traditionally grown vegetables, free range eggs
and lemon curd, jams, pickles and chutneys.

FARMERS' MARKETS

Clitheroe Farmers' Market

Clitheroe Auction Market,
The Ribblesdale Centre BB7 1QD
01200 423325
Monthly farmers' market.

Colne Farmers' Market

Market Square, Market Street Car Park, Market
Hall, Colne BB7 1QD
01282 661240
Takes place on the third Saturday monthly.

Fleetwood Farmers' Market

Adelaide Street, Fleetwood, Lancashire FY7 6AB
01253 771651
www.fleetwoodmarket.com
Held on the third Friday of every month.

Great Eccleston Farmers' Market

Market Square, High Street, Great Eccleston,
Preston PR3 0YB
01995 670386
Third Wednesday of every month.

Lancaster Farmers' Market

Market Square, Lancaster, Lancashire LA1 1HU
01524 582158
On the second Wednesday monthly.

Lytham St Annes Farmers' Market

Pleasure Island, Lytham St Annes,
Lancashire FY8 1LS
01995 670386
First Thursday monthly.

Merchant of Hoghton Farmers' Market

Hoghton Tower, Hoghton, Preston PR5 0SH
01254 852986
Held on the third Sunday of every month (except
July, which is one week earlier than usual).

Penwortham Farmers' Market

St Mary's Church, Cop Lane, Penwortham, Preston,
Lancashire
01772 751015
Held on the first Saturday of every month.

Poulton Farmers' Market

St Chads Church Hall, Poulton le Fylde, Preston,
Lancashire FY6 7LT
01253 883470
Held on the fourth Saturday monthly.

Ramsbottom Farmers' Market

Civic Hall, Ramsbottom, Lancashire
0161 253 5974
Held on the second Sunday monthly.

Rossendale Farmers' Market

Premises of Airtours, Helmshore
01706244230
Held on the first Sunday of each month.

Salwick Farmers' Market

Cunliffe Fold Farm, Blackleach Lane, Salwick,
Preston PR4 0RY
01772 690622
Every Saturday.

Scarisbrick Farmers' Market

Scarisbrick Village Hall, Scarisbrick
01704 880623
Held on the second Tuesday every month.

Uppermill/Oldham Farmers' Market
Saddleworth Museum, High Street, Uppermill,
Oldham Ol3 6HS
01457 873590
Held on the second Saturday monthly.

EATING PLACES

The Bay Horse Inn
Forton, Lancashire LA2 0HR
01524 791 204
www.bayhorseinn.com
Restaurant using local produce.

The Derby Arms
Chipping Lane, Thornley, near Longridge,
Preston PR3 2NB
01772 782623
Restaurant and public house sourcing local ingredients.

Dunscar and Lewis
106 Southport New Road, Tarleton, Preston,
Lancashire PR4 6HY
01772 811111
Restaurant. Fine foods, light lunches and refreshments.

The Eagle and Child
Bispham Green, Near Parbold L40 3SG
01257 462297
Selling local real ales and quality meals.

Garstang Golf Club and Country Hotel
Bowgreave, Garstang, Preston PR3 1YE
01995 600100
Hotel and restaurant serving locally sourced produce.

The Gibbon Bridge Hotel
Chipping, Forest of Bowland, Preston,
Lancashire PR3 2TQ
01995 61456
www.gibbon-bridge.co.uk
Locally sourced ingredients and on site bakery.

The Green Man
Silk Mill Lane, Inglewhite, Preston PR3 2LP
01995 640 292
Public house with restaurant selling homemade cakes, biscuits, sweet and savoury pies.

The Longridge Restaurant
104-106 Higher Road, Longridge, Preston PR3 3SY
01772 784969 www.simplyheathcotes.com
Fine-dining restaurant run by innovative chef Paul Heathcote.

Millstone at Mellor
Church Lane, Mellor, Blackburn BB2 7JR
01254 813333
www.shirehotels.co.uk
Village inn and restaurant sourcing quality local produce.

Northcote Manor
Northcote Road, Langho, Blackburn BB6 8BE
01254 240 555
www.northcotemanor.com
Nigel Howarth's menus, featuring regional producers and growers.

Pendle Heritage Centre
Park Hill, Barrowford, near Nelson BB9 6JQ
01282 661702
www.htnw.co.uk
A gallery and parlour shop. Tourist outlet.

RSPB Leighton Moss Nature Reserve
Silverdale, Carnforth, Lancashire LA5 0SW
01524 701601
www.rspb.org.uk
Tearoom sourcing local produce.

Seniors Fish Bar
106 Normoss Road, Blackpool FY3 8QP
Fish bar and restaurant.

Springfield House Hotel
Wheel Lane, Pilling, Preston, Lancashire PR3 6HL
01253 790301
www.springfieldhouse.uk.com
Hotel restaurant serving quality local produce.

The Station
c/o Bispham Green, Near Parbold,
Lancashire L40 3SG
01257 462297
Café with breads and pastries baked on site.

The Stork Inn
Conder Green, near Lancaster LA2 0AN
01524 751 234
Part of the Mortal Man Inns group. Country inn sourcing local ingredients.

Thyme at the Sirloin Inn
Station Road, Hoghton, Preston PR5 0DD
012548 52293
www.thyme-restaurant.co.uk
Restaurant using locally sourced ingredients.

Ye Horns Inn
Horns Inn, Goosnargh, Preston
01772 865 230
info@yehornsinn.co.uk
Public house and restaurant selling homemade puddings on the menu.

GREATER MANCHESTER

Local Food First Greater Manchester
Contact: Jennifer Lambert
West Lancashire Technology Management
Centre, Moss Lane View,
Skelmersdale WN8 9TN
01695 732 734
jlambert@nwff.co.uk
www.nwff.co.uk

FRUIT AND VEGETABLES

Unicorn Co-operative Grocery
89 Albany Road, Chorlton, Manchester M21 0BN
www.unicorn-grocery.co.uk
Fresh wholesome snacks and delicacies, organic
range of whole foods, beers, cider and wines. Wide
range of fruit and veg.

BAKERY AND CONFECTIONERY

The Baker
Gatley, Greater Manchester
0161 238 4348
Award-winner for Best Overall Dessert 2004
for Chocolate Tart.
High quality bakers and confectioners.

Barbakan Delicatessen Limited
67-71 Manchester Road, Chorlton Cum Hardy,
Manchester M21 9PW
0161 881 7053
www.barbakan-deli.co.uk
Delicatessen with speciality craft bakery.

Route Ginger
53 Clarendon Road, Sale M33 2DY
07788 668956, 0161 969 4116
Homemade cakes and preserves.

Sandy's Bakehouse
Unit 1 and 2 Montford Enterprise Centre,
West Ashton Street, Salford M5 2XS
0161 737 2700
Bakery and confectionery.

Slattery Patissier and Chocolatier
197 Bury New Road, Whitefield M45 6GE
0161 767 9303
www.slattery.co.uk
Reputable and popular patissier and chocolatier.

William Santus and Co Ltd
The Toffee Works, Dorning Street, Wigan WN1 1HE
01942 246464
www.uncle-joes.com
Manufacturers of traditional high quality
confectionery specialising in Uncle Joe's Mint Balls.

MEATS

Andrews Continental Delicacies
Unit 2-4 Muslin Street, Salford,
Greater Manchester M5 4NF
0161 745 8449
Handmade continental style sausages.

Bennetts Quality Meats Ltd
28 Princes Parade, Bury,
Greater Manchester BL9 0QL
0161 761 1501
martyn@bennett561.freeserve.co.uk
High quality butchers, member of Q Guild of
Butchers.

FB Taylor and Son
138 Northenden Road, Sale,
Greater Manchester M33 3HE
0161 9733480
taylors.butchers@ntworld.com
Butchers making own sausages and burgers.
Member of Guild of Q Butchers.

Frasers Butchers Ltd
272 Rishton Lane, Great Lever, Bolton BL3 2EH
01204 523278

Gabbotts Farm (Retail) Limited
Chaddock Lane, Astley, Tyldesley,
Greater Manchester M29 7JY
01942 885320
www.gabbottsfarm.co.uk
Quality chain of high street butchers.

Home Farm
Haigh, Wigan, Greater Manchester WN2 1PD
01942 831058
www.forsterorganicmeats.co.uk
Organic beef and lamb reared naturally on grass.

Noel Chadwicks
Wellington Place, High Street, Standish WN6 0HD
01257 421137
www.noelchadwick.co.uk
Butchers, deli and café. Member of Guild of Q
Butchers.

Tittertons (Stockport)
24 Princes Street, Stockport,
Greater Manchester SK1 1SE
0161 480 6905
Family butchers, famous for high quality home
produced sausages, dry-cured bacon and cooked
meats.

WH Frost (Butchers) Limited
12-14 Chorlton Place, Wilbraham Road,
Chorlton M21 9AQ
0161 881 8172
Traditional quality family butchers.

BEVERAGES

Raw Juice Company
Goyt Mill, Upper Hibbert Lane, Marple,
Stockport SK6 7HX
0161 427 7800
www.rawjuice.biz
Freshly squeezed citrus fruit juices and prepared
fruit salads.

Millstone Brewery
Unit 4, Vale Mill, Micklehurst Road,
Mossley OL5 9JL
01457 835 835
Real ale brewery using traditional malt and hops.

Vimto Soft Drinks
Laurel House, Woodlands Park, Ashton Road,
Newton le Willows WA12 0HH
01925 222 222
www.vimto.co.uk

SAUCES

Seasoners Fine Foods Ltd
69 Acorn Centre, Off Barry Street, Derker,
Oldham OL1 3NE
0161 627 2027
picklers@talk21.com
Pickles, preserves and sauces using traditional
methods and fresh ingredients.

VINEGARS / OILS

Gift of Oil
The Enterprize Centre, Washington Street,
Bolton BL3 5EY
01204 559555
www.thegiftofoil.co.uk
Bringing extra virgin olive oil and balsamic vinegar
to the region.

FARM SHOPS

Redhouse Farm Shop and Tearoom
Redhouse Farm, Redhouse Lane,
Dunham Massey WA14 5RL
0161 9413480
www.redhousefarm.co.uk
Fresh produce, cheese, homemade cakes and pies.

Park Farm
Walmersley, Bury, Greater Manchester BL9 5NP
01706 823577
Family run farm shop and tearoom, using their own
dairy and beef produce. Regular stall at the local
farmers' markets.

BOX SCHEME

Northern Harvest
Kenyon Hall Farm, Winwick Lane, Croft,
Warrington WA3 7ED
0845 6023309
www.kenyonhall.co.uk
Home delivery service for finest regional produce.

FARMERS' MARKETS

Altrincham Farmers' Market
Market Street, Altrincham, Greater Manchester
0161 9414261
First Friday of every month.

**Ashton under Lyne Farmers' and
Producers' Market**
Ashton Market Ground, Bow Street,
Ashton under Lyne
0161 3423268
marketmanhik@ashton-under-lyne.com
Last Sunday of every month.

Manchester Farmers' Market
Piccadilly Gardens, Manchester
0161 2347356
Second Saturday and the preceding Friday of every
month.

**Ramsbottom Farmers', Producers' and
Craft Market**
Civic Hall
0161 253 5974
Held on the second Sunday monthly.

Rochdale Farmers' Market
Rochdale Market, 33 Market Place, Rochdale,
Lancashire OL16 1EB
01706 710400
Held on the first Sunday monthly.

Wigan Farmers' Market
The Galleries, New Market Street, Wigan WN1 1PX
01942 708101
Held on the first Tuesday of every month.

EATING PLACES

The Bridge
58 Bridge Street, Manchester M3 3BW
0161 834 0242
Gastropub using local produce.

Choice Bar and Restaurant
Castle Quay, Castlefield, Manchester M15 4NT
0161 833 3400
Manchester Restaurant of the Year 2003-2004
specialising in contemporary regional recipes using
fine North West produce.

Isinglass English Dining Rooms
46 Flixton Road, Manchester M41 5AB
0161 749 8400
Entirely English dishes made from local farm
produce and meats.

Loves Saves The Day
Smithfield Buildings, Oldham Street,
Manchester M4 1LE
0161 832 0777
and 345 Deansgate, Manchester M3 4LG
0161 834 2266
www.lovesavestheday.co.uk
Quality delicatessen and café specialising in local
produce.

Le Mont Restaurant
Urbis, Cathedral Gardens, Manchester M4 3BG
0161 605 8282
www.urbis.org.uk
Restaurant specialising in robert Kisby's cuisine.

Urbis
Cathedral Gardens, Manchester M4 3BG
0161 605 8200
www.urbis.org.uk
A visitor attraction devoted to the study of urban
cultures. Eating places within.

The White Hart Inn
51 Stockport Road, Lydgate, Saddleworth,
Oldham OL4 4JJ
01457872566
www.thewhitehart.co.uk
Menus using top quality produce.

MERSEYSIDE

Local Food First Merseyside
Contact: Suzanne Shufflebotham
West Lancashire Technology Management
Centre, Moss Lane View,
Skelmersdale WN8 9TN
01695 732 734
sshufflebotham@nwff.co.uk
www.nwff.co.uk

DAIRY

Brimstage Ice Cream
Oak Cottage, Blakeley Road, Raby Mere,
Merseyside CH63 0NA
0151 334 0898
www.lyneandhartley.com
Ice creams from Guernsey milk and sorbets.

FRUIT AND VEGETABLES

Church Farm Organics
Church Farm, Church Lane, Thurstaston, Wirral,
Merseyside CH61 0HW
0151 648 7838
www.churchfarm.co.uk
Large variety of homegrown organic produce,
including fruit and veg. Farm shop including coffee
shop.

Claremont Farm
Old Clatterbridge Road, Bebington, Wirral,
Merseyside CH63 4JB
0151 334 1906
Strawberry and asparagus growers, supplying
outlets. Farm shop selling a range of speciality
products.

Fir Tree Farm
Kings Moss, Crank, St Helens,
Merseyside WA11 8RG
01744 892277
Freshly grown produce. Farm shop.

Flavourfresh Salads Limited
Aldergrove Centre, Marsh Road, Banks,
Southport PR9 8DX
01704 232223
www.flavourfresh.co.uk,
High quality tomatoes with great flavour.

Organic Direct
57 Blundell Street, Liverpool, Merseyside L1 0AJ
0151 707 6949
Box scheme delivering organic fruit and vegetables.

BAKERY AND CONFECTIONERY

Born and Bred
3 Coronation Buildings, Wallasey Road, Liscard,
Wirral CH45 4NE
0151 637 2482
Artisan bread makers.

Chocolate Garden
248 Brookhurst Avenue, Wirral CH62 9EX
0151 327 7247
Handmade chocolates.

Dafnas Cheesecake Factory
240 Smithdown Road, Liverpool L15 5AH
0151 733 7808
www.dafna.co.uk
Homemade cakes.

John Pimblett and Sons
College Bakery, College Street, St Helens,
Merseyside WA10 1TP
01744 455500
www.pimbletts.co.uk
Craftsman bakers, confectioners and pastrycooks.
Unique celebration and wedding cakes Also shops
in Widnes, Rainford, Whiston and around
St Helens.

M Ray Limited
39-45 High Street, Prescot, Merseyside L34 6HF
0151 426 6148
www.mrays.com
High class bakers, special Christmas and traditional
English puddings.

The Magic Dessert Co Ltd
Oak Cottage, Blakeley Road, Raby Mere,
Merseyside CH63 0NA
0151 334 0898
lyndeandhartley@freeola.com
Desserts.

Mary's Homemade Cakes
3 Weatherstones Mews, Hanns Hall Road,
Willaston CH64 7TF
0151 336 4720
www.maryscakes.co.uk
Quality homemade cakes using only the finest local
ingredients.

Sarjeants Confectionery
28 Birkenhead Road, Hoylake, Wirral,
Merseyside CH47 3BW
0151 632 2399
www.sarjeants.co.uk
Handmade Belgium chocolates and truffles.

MEATS

Brough Butchers
Birkdale, Southport, Merseyside
01704 567 073
581 Liverpool Road, Ainsdale,
Southport PR8 3LU
01704 567073
366 Chapel Lane, Formby L37 4DU
01704 872 075
www.broughs.com
Winner of Best Bacon and Overall Best Cured
Meat Award 2004. A range of high quality
meats.

Callaghan G and Son
8 Central Square, Maghull, Merseyside L31 0AE
0151 526 9345
Quality guild butchers.

Edge and Sons Butchers
61 Newchester Road, New Ferry,
Merseyside CH62 1AB
0151 645 3044
www.traditionalmeat.com
Rare breed butcher established in 1844.

J and J Forster
Shoots Delph Farm, Moss Bank Road,
St Helens WA11 7NU
01942 831058
www.fosterorganicmeats.co.uk
Farming family producing quality organic beef and
lamb.

Morpro Oakwell Brand
Holt Lane, Netherley Industrial Estate, Netherley,
Liverpool L27 2YB
0151 487 3222
www.spoilt4choice.com
Sausages, black puddings and bacon. Oakwell's
award-winning black puddings.

Muffs of Bromborough
5-7 Allport Lane, Bromborough, Wirral,
Merseyside CH62 7HH
0151 334 2002
www.muffsonline.co.uk
Award-winning sausages and meat products using
locally reared meats.

Worrall House Farm Larder
Worrall House Farm, Flatmans Lane, Downholland,
Merseyside
0151 526 0323
www.freshpork.co.uk
Home produced pork products and other locally
sourced meats.

SEAFOOD

Southport Potted Shrimps
66 Station Road, Banks Village,
Southport PR9 8BB
01704 229266
www.pottedshrimp.com
Runner-up for Traditional Speciality and Best
Potted Shrimps 2004.
Traditional potted shrimps.

BEVERAGES

Bellew's Coffee and Tea Co
5 Hope Way, Liverpool L8 7PH

Punch Brew Co
49 Queensway, Moss Bank, St Helens,
Merseyside WA11 7BY
07733108147
Traditional herbal punch.

Robert Cain Brewery Ltd
Stanhope Street, Liverpool, Merseyside L8 5XJ
0151 709 8734
www.cains.co.uk
Liverpool's 150-year-old brewery.

Wapping Brewery (and Baltic Fleet)
33 Wapping, Liverpool L1 8DQ
0151 709 3116
Brewery, Baltic Fleet pub and restaurant.

SAUCES

Chinese Chef Foods
Musker Street, Great Crosby, Liverpool,
Merseyside L23 0UB
0151 931 3200
Frozen cooking sauces and bottled dipping sauces.

Edmund Barton Ltd
Lascelles Street, St Helens, Merseyside WA9 1BA
01744 22593
www.bartonspickles.com
Traditional and innovative pickles, sauces and
chutneys.

SPICES AND HERBS

Seasoned Pioneers
Unit 101, Sumners Road, Brunswick Business
Park, Liverpool L3 4BJ
0151 709 9330
www.seasonedpioneers.co.uk
Winner of Best Ingredient for Ras-al-Hanout
spice blend. Authentic spice blends and
seasonings.

FARM SHOPS

Acorn Venture
Depot Road, Kirkby
0151 548 1524
www.acornfarm.co.uk
An urban farm selling a range of home produced
goods.

Church Farm Organics
Church Farm, Church Lane, Thurstaston, Wirral,
Merseyside CH61 0HW
0151 648 7838
www.churchfarm.co.uk
Large variety of homegrown organic produce, including
fruit and veg. Farm shop including coffee shop.

Church View Farm Shop
Southport Road, Lydiate, Merseyside
0151 250 2673
Local homegrown produce.

Dale Farm
51 Oldfield Road, Heswall, Wirral CH60 6SN
0151 342 7819
Award-winning day centre producing own organic
vegetables, honey and plants.

Fir Tree Farm
Kings Moss, Crank, St Helens,
Merseyside WA11 8RG
01744 892277
Freshly grown produce. Farm shop.

Huntsbrook Farm and Shop
East Lane, Homer Green, Thornton,
Merseyside L29 3EA
0151 924 2727
Farm shop selling range of regional and local
produce.

Yew Tree Farm Shop
Yew Tree Farm, Lower Road, Halewood,
Liverpool L26 3UA
0151 487 5165
www.yew-tree-farm.com
Home produced vegetables, free range chicken,
turkes and lamb.

Worrall House Farm Larder
Worrall House Farm, Flatmans Lane, Downholland,
Merseyside
0151 526 0323
www.farmerteds.com
Home produced pork products and other locally
sourced meats. Also farmerteds children's farm
onsite.

BOX SCHEME

J and J Forster
Shoots Delph Farm, Moss Bank Road,
St Helens WA11 7NU
01942 831058
www.fosterorganicmeats.co.uk
Farming family producing quality organic beef and lamb.

FARMERS' MARKETS

Bootle Farmers' Market
Next to Bootle Library, Liverpool
0151 934 4283
Held on the third Thursday every month.

Liverpool Farmers' Market
Outside TJ Hughes, London Road, Liverpool L3 8JA
0151 233 2165, 0151 708 948
Held on the first and third Saturday of every month.

Maghull Farmers' Market
Central Square, Eastway, Maghull, Merseyside
0151 934 4283
First Sunday monthly.

Southport Farmers' Market
King Street, Southport, Merseyside
0151 934 4283
Held on the last Thursday monthly.

Wirral Farmers' Market
New Ferry Village Hall, Grove Street,
New Ferry CH62 5HN
0151 643 1393
Held on the second Saturday monthly.

EATING PLACES

60 Hope Street
Liverpool L1 9BZ
0151 707 6060
www.60hopestreet.com
Restaurant using high quality local ingredients.

Baltic Fleet (and Wapping Brewery)
33 Wapping, Liverpool L1 8DQ
0151 709 3116
Restaurant.

Blackburne House Café
Blackburne Place, Hope Street, Liverpool L8 7PE
0151 709 4356
www.blackburnehouse.co.uk
Café, local produce where possible.

Everyman Bistro
13 Hope St, Liverpool L1 9BH
0151 708 9545
Local produce sourced for menus.

Fairways Restaurant
Houghwood Golf Course, Billinge Hill, Crank Road, Crank, St Helens
01744 894 754
www.houghwoodgolfcourse.co.uk
Modern British cuisine dedicated to using local produce.

Garrett's
2a Bromborough Road, Wirral CH63 7RE
0151 645 7199
www.garrettsrestaurant.com
Restaurant sourcing local and organic produce where possible.

London Carriage Works
Hope Street, Liverpool L1
0151 705 2222
www.hopestreethotel.co.uk
High quality dining restaurant and hotel.

Number 7 Café and Deli
7-15 Falkner Street, off Hope Street, Liverpool, Merseyside L8 7PU
0151 709 9633
Excellent range of regional foods.

The Other Place Bistro and Deli
43 Allerton Road, Liverpool, Merseyside L18 2DD
0151 724 1234
Fresh quality food and original menus.

The Other Place Bistro
29a Hope Street, Liverpool L1
0151 707 7888
Fresh quality food and original menus.

The Red Cat
8 Red Cat Lane, Crank, St Helens, Merseyside WA11 8RJ
01744 882422
Country pub serving locally sourced contemporary food.

Station Brasserie and Bar
24-28 Hamilton Street, Birkenhead, Wirral CH41 1AL
0151 647 1047
www.sleepstation.co.uk
Innovative brasserie and bar with five individual hotel bedrooms.

Racquet Club Hotel and Ziba Restaurant
5 Chapel Street, Liverpool L3 9AG
www.racquetclub.org.uk
Highly rated modern food incorporating local
produce in an innovative way.

The Warehouse Brasserie
30 West Street, Southport PR8 1QN
01704 544662
www.warehouse-brasserie.co.uk
Fine dining restaurant dedicated to sourcing local
and regional food, home to Merseyside Young Chef
of the Year 2002 and 2003. Also producers of fine
artisan breads.

CHESHIRE

Made in Cheshire
Contact: Jane Casson
Room 251, County Hall,
Chester CH1 1SF
01244 603 822
jane.casson@cheshire.gov.uk
www.madeincheshire.com

DAIRY AND EGGS

Cheshire Farm Ice Cream
Drumlan Hall, Newton Lane, Tattenhall,
Cheshire CH3 9NE
01829 770995
www.cheshirefarmicecream.co.uk
Made with only fresh milk from the farm, double
cream and top quality ingredients. A range of
flavours and real fruit sorbets. Open to the public.

Delamere Dairy Ltd
Yew Tree Farm, Bexton Lane, Knutsford,
Cheshire WA16 9BH
01565 750 528
info@delameredairy.co.uk
Goat milk, yoghurts, butter and cheeses.

Dunham Massey Farm Ice Cream
Ash Farm, Station Road, Dunham Massey,
Altrincham WA14 5SG
0161 9281230
20 flavours of real dairy ice cream, plus four sorbet
flavours sold in the farm shop and from farmers'
markets.

FG Leigh and Sons
Manor Farm, Bypass Road, Dunkirk, Chester,
Cheshire CH1 6LZ
01244 851223
Producer of high quality eggs using feed made
from homegrown cereals.

Godfrey C Williams and Son
9-11 The Square, Sandbach, Cheshire CW11 1AP
01270 762817
Blended speciality cheeses.

Granellis Cream Ices Macclesfield Ltd
74 Newton Street, Macclesfield, Cheshire SK11 6RJ
01625 424391
Ice cream manufacturer of 40 flavours.

HS Bourne
The Bank, Malpas, Cheshire SY12 7AL
01948 770214
www.hsbourne.co.uk
Winner of the Traditional Regional Speciality
Award 2004. Handmade farmhouse Cheshire
cheeses.

Hilly Billy Ice Cream
Blaze Farm, Wildboarclough, Macclesfield,
Cheshire SK11 0BL
01260 227229
katy@hillybilly.co.uk
Ice cream parlour, tearoom and nature trail.

IF Lloyd
Leadgate Farm, Huxley, Chester, Cheshire CH3 9BT
01829 781376
Egg producer.

JS Bailey
Calveley Mill, Nantwich Road, Calveley, Tarpoley,
Cheshire CW6 9JW
01829 262900
jsbaileycheese@lineone.net
Cheese, wholesale.

Joseph Heler Ltd
Laurels Farm, Crewe Road, Hatherton,
Nantwich CW5 7PE
01270 841 500
www.joseph-heler.co.uk
Large range of cheeses and whey products.

Lewis Brothers Ice Cream
Lewis Square, Lilford Street, Warrington,
Cheshire WA5 5LJ
01925 632994
sales@lewisbros.lls.com
Premium Italian style ice cream in several flavours.

Messrs ET Griffiths
Kinderton Lodge Farm, Middlewich, Cheshire
01606 832 386
d_l_griffiths@hotmail.com
Free range eggs.

Messrs J and E Heler
Half Moon Farm, Blakenhall, Nantwich,
Cheshire CW5 7WR
01270 841237
l.edward@heler.freeserve.co.uk
Goat milk fresh or frozen. Home-reared goat, beef,
lamb and pork. Meat subject to availability.

Nicholls of Parkgate
The Parade, Parkgate, Neston CH64 6SA
0151 336 1274
gelatoun@hotmail.com
Ice cream manufacturer and retailer.

Poplars Farm Free Range Eggs
Poplars Farm, Barbers Lane, Antrobus, Northwich,
Cheshire CW9 6JP
01565 777 543
Farm shop selling wholesale and free range eggs.

Ravens Oak Dairy
Burland Farm, Wrexham Road, Burland,
Nantwich CW5 8ND
01270 524624
www.butlerscheeses.co.uk
Winner of Best Cheese and Overall Best Dairy
for their Goat Cheese. Handmade speciality
fresh and mould-rinded cheeses, some
organic.

Snugburys Jersey Ice Cream
Park Farm, Hurleston, Nantwich CW5 6BU
01270 624830
www.snugburys.co.uk
A large variety of flavours including raspberry ripple
and damson and gin. Wholesale orders welcome.
Open to the public.

Tiresford Guernsey Gold
Tiresford Farm, Tarporley CW6 9LY
01829 734 080
Live yoghurt made using the farm's award-winning
herd of Guernsey's milk. Available in four flavours.

BAKERY AND CONFECTIONERY

**Arthur Chatwin Ltd Bakers and
Confectioners**
4 Market Street, Nantwich, Cheshire CW5 5DJ
01270 625 127
www.chatwins.co.uk
Craft bakery producing award-winning bread and
confectionery for its 20 retail outlets.

Corby Chocolates
Firwood Cottage, Mottram Road, Alderley Edge,
Cheshire SK9 7DW
01625 865 671
ruth.samuels@lightninginternet.co.uk
Specialising in luxury handmade champagne
truffles and other flavours. Packaged for delis and
other high quality outlets.

Devonshire Bakery
1 High Street, Frodsham, Cheshire WA6 7AH
01928 788619
www.devonshire-bakery.co.uk
Bakery selling celebration cakes, pies, breads and
seasonal chocolate.

Harrisons Bakers and Confectioners
5 Queens Court, Sadler Road, Winsford,
Cheshire CW7 2BD
01606 591444
Bakery, confectioners and delicatessen.

Le Chocolatier
8 Barrowmore Estate, Great Barrow, near Chester,
Cheshire CH3 7JA
01829 741010
Manufacturers of fine chocolates, truffles, fresh
cream and pralines.

Mary's Cakes
3 Weatherstones Mews, Hanns Hall Road,
Willaston, South Wirral CH64 7TF
0151 336 4720
www.maryscakes.co.uk
Homemade cakes using local farm eggs and butter.
Fruitcakes and also Christmas puddings are a
speciality.

Stanways Bakery
Knutsford Road, Antrobus, Northwich,
Cheshire CW9 6JW
01606 891467
Wholesale.

FRUIT AND VEGETABLES

Abbey Leys Farm
Peacock Lane, High Legh, Near Knutsford,
Cheshire WA16 6NS
01925 753465
www.abbeyleys.co.uk
Farm shop selling organic free range eggs,
potatoes and vegetables.

Cherry Orchard Farm
Abbey Lane, Oakmere, Near Northwich,
Cheshire CW8 2HN
01606 882039
Asparagus May to June.

Cherry Tree Farm Shop

Cherry Tree Farm, School Lane, Manley,
Frodsham WA6 9DY
01928 740301
cherrytreemanley@btopenworld.com
Homegrown Cheshire new and winter main crop
potatoes. Seasonal vegetables and produce
throughout the year, such as fruit, eggs and wild
bird food.

D and J Rathbone

Cuttleford Farm, Newcastle Road, Astbury,
Congleton, Cheshire CW12 4SD
01260 272499
Homegrown fruit and vegetables sold in our own
farm shop and local wholesale markets and pubs.

DJ Lowe and Partners

Shanty Farm, Byley, Middlewich,
Cheshire CW10 9NG
01606 832133
Growers of a wide range of vegetables and
potatoes, freshly picked every day for the farm
shop, complimented by other local produce.

David Latham

Brindley Lea Hall, Nantwich, Cheshire CW5 8HX
01270 524239
Farming/agricultural contracting. Potatoes and eggs
are produced.

Eddisbury Fruit Farm

Yeld Lane, Kelsall, Cheshire CW6 0TE
01829 751 300
m.m.haworth@btinternet.com
Winner of Best Soft Drink Award 2004 for
Apple and Blackcurrant Juice. Fruit and fruit
juice producers.

Kenyon Hall Farm

Winwick Lane, Croft, Warrington WA3 7ED
01925 763 646
www.kenyonhall.co.uk
Pick your own quality fruit and vegetables and farm
shop.

Oakcroft Organic Gardens

Cross O' Th' Hill, Malpas SY14 8DH
01948 860213
An organic market garden selling vegetables and
fruit.

SD and GW Lowe

Field House Farm, Lostock Gralam, Northwich,
Cheshire CW9 7TH
077788581070
Beef and cereal farm, producing 5 acres of mixed
vegetables for retail sale.

MEAT

Alan Jackson Butchers

27 London Road, Alderley Edge SK9 7JT
01625 583 143
www.alanjacksonbutchers.co.uk
Varieties of sausage including a gluten-free
sausage.

Baileys Turkeys

Dairy House Farm, Chester Road, Tabley,
Knutsford WA16 0PN
01565 632174
sales@baileysturkeys.co.uk
Fresh turkeys and turkey meat products.

CS Austin

132 Northgate Street, Chester CH1 2HT
01244 320734
www.caustin.co.uk
Butchers selling locally produced meats and
delicatessen.

Ernest W Edge and Son

54-56 Handbridge, Chester CH4 7JP
01244 675156
Butchers, game dealers and deli.

JE and H Roach

Chapel Farm, Hatherton, Nantwich,
Cheshire CW5 7QT
01270 841294
Pigs reared for the freezer and hog roasts.

H Clewlow Butchers

8 Pepper Street, Nantwich CW5 5AB
01270 625366
www.clewlows.co.uk
Specialist in sausages, pies, local beef, pork and
lamb.

Harrisons Poultry

Warrington Road, Antrobus, Northwich,
Cheshire CW9 6JB
01606 891285
www.britishpoussin.co.uk
Once a small family business, now grown to
become the UK's largest grower and processor of
poussin. Supplier to all the major UK retailers and
some small catering butchers.

Hopkinsons of Lymm

7 The Cross, Lymm, Cheshire WA13 0HR
01925 758016
joanne.hopkinson@btopenworld.com
Butchers.

Lama Load Lamb
Common Barn Farm, Smith Lane, Rainow,
Macclesfield SK10 5JX
01625 574878
g.greengrass@hotmail.com
Home produced lamb available.

Lamb from Audlem
Fields Farm, Green Lane, Audlem, Crewe,
Cheshire CW3 0ES
01270 811070
chrislewis@globalnet.co.uk
Half prime lambs either fresh or frozen. Vegetable
and soft fruit honesty stall at side of Lock 9 on
Shropshire Union Canal.

Organic On The Hill
Butterlands Farm, Wincle, Macclesfield,
Cheshire SK11 0QL
01260 227672
www.organiconthehill.co.uk
Home-reared organic beef, lamb and pork
produce.

S Vaughan Family Butchers
Wood Lane, Penyfford, Chester CH4 0JN
01244 543102
ngaio23@btopenworld.com
Award-winning butchers. National sausage
champion. Supplier of local farm produced beef,
lamb and pork.

Snape Farm
Snape Lane, Weston, Crewe CW2 5NB
01270 820208
jean@snapefarm.fsnet.co.uk
Traditional Aberdeen Angus beef.

Sugar Brook Farm
Mobberley Road, Ashley, Altrincham WA14 3QB
0161 9280879
Homegrown organic lamb, potatoes and
vegetables.

Tatton Park
Knutsford, Cheshire WA16 6QN
01829 534 400
Prime venison, pork, rare breed lamb and rabbit.

Tittertons
24 Princess Street, Stockport SK1 1SE
0161 480 6905
Quality guild butchers.

CURED MEATS

The Cheshire Smokehouse Ltd
Vost Farm, Morley Green, Wilmslow,
Cheshire SK9 5NU
01625 548499
www.cheshiresmokehouse.co.uk
Curers and smokers. On site production of dry-cured
bacons and hams (using local pork), smoked salmon
and other meats and fish. Bespoke hampers all year
round. Speciality food shop and café.

BEVERAGES

Beartown Brewery Ltd
Bromlwy House, Spindle Street, Congleton,
Cheshire CW12 1QN
01260 299 964
www.beartownbrewery.co.uk
Small independent brewery with pub estate.

Coach House Brewing Company Ltd
Wharf Street, Howley, Warrington,
Cheshire WA1 2DQ
01925 232 800
djbcoachhouse@hotmail.com
Brewers of traditional hand-crafted cask conditioned
fine ales.

Khean Brewing Co Ltd
4 Royle Park, Royle Street, Congleton,
Cheshire CW12 1JJ
01260 272 144
Brewers of several cask and bottle conditioned ales
for supply to both local and not so local free trade,
using traditional malts, hops and Cheshire water.

Old Creamery Bottling Company
Paradise Brewery, The Old Creamery, Wrenbury,
Cheshire CW5 8EX
01270 780916
john@gillmorgan.go-plus.net
Brewing and bottling of beers.

Storm Brewing Company
2 Waterside, Macclesfield SK11 7HJ
01625 431 234
thompsonhugh@talk21.com
Brewers of beer supplied to the trade and general
public in casks and bottles.

Weetwood Ales Ltd
Weetwood Grange, Weetwood, Tarporley,
Cheshire CW6 0NQ
01829 752377

SPECIALITY FOODS

The Cheese Shop
116 Northgate Street, Chester CH1 2HT
01244 346240
www.chestercheeseshop.com
Promotes Cheshire, Northern and British cheeses
and also sells chutneys, biscuits, wines and ciders.

The Cheshire Smokehouse
Vost Farm, Morley Green, Wilmslow,
Cheshire SK9 5NU
01625 548 499
Renowned range of products including dry-cured
bacon and hams, smoked fish and much more.
Nearly 100 years of experience.

The Housekeeper's Store
Tatton Park, Knutsford WA16 6QN
01625 534 422
www.tattonpark.org.uk
Speciality food shop offering Tatton's own prime
venison, bacon and pork produce. Farmhouse
cheeses and a variety of traditional fine foods from
farm, estate and local producers.

James's
Unit 6, Guy Lane, Waverton, Chester,
Cheshire CH3 7NB
01244 335295
Sandwich shop and delicatessen.

Masons Gourmet Foods
Thornhill, Fluin Lane, Frodsham,
Cheshire WA6 7QU
01928 733 159
Cakes, puddings and chocolates.

Organicfair
43 St James Street, Off Hoole Way, Chester,
Cheshire CH1 3EX
01244 400 158
www.organicfair.co.uk
Organically certified, fairtrade and natural products.

Spicetech
15 Buxton Road, Disley SK12 2DZ
01663 766900
www.sausagemaking.co.uk
Sausage-making kits.

Sullivan and Allan Fine Foods
10a Faulkner Street, Hoole, Chester,
Cheshire CH2 3BD
01244 340505
mags@delicat.fsbusiness.co.uk
Delicatessen and outside catering.

Taylor's Speciality Foods Ltd
Canal Side, Tattenhall Road, Tattenhall,
Cheshire CH3 9BD
01829 771166
www.taylors-foods.com
Wide range of mustards, condiments, preserves and
sauces.

PREPARED FOODS

Marton Coffee House and Brasserie
Manchester Road, Marton, Macclesfield
Cheshire SK11 9HF
01260 224785
Freshly made soups and ready cooked meals.

Essential Cuisine
Unit 4 Innovation House, Browning Way, Woodford
Park Industrial Estate, Winsford, Cheshire CW7 2RH
0870 0501133
www.essentialcuisine.com
Producers of a top quality range of stocks and juices.

Eazy Cuizine
69 King Street, Knutsford WA16 6DX
01565 653244
www.eazycuizine.com
Producer of quality blast frozen ready meals using
fresh local ingredients wherever possible.

Natural Larder
C/O Marton Coffee House and Brasserie,
Church Farm, Manchester Road, Marton,
Macclesfield SK11 9HF
01625 583 050
Award-winner for Best Ready Meal, Sauce or
Soup 2004 for Moussaka. Handmade dishes
sold under the Natural Larder brand, as well
as served at Marton Coffee House.

PRESERVES

Combermere Abbey Cottages
Combermere Abbey, Whitchurch,
Cheshire SY13 4AJ
01948 662 876
www.combermereabbey.co.uk
A selection of homemade preserves – jams, jellies
and chutneys using fruit from the fruit tree maze
and gardens at Combermere Abbey.

Farmhouse Products
Childs Lane, Brownlow, Congleton,
Cheshire CW12 4TG
01477 500660
Quality gift foods including preserves, chutney,
pickles, sauces and condiments, marmalades,
curds, tea, coffee, confectionery and cakes.

SPICES AND HERBS

Lion Salt Works Trust
Ollershaw Lane, Marston, Northwich,
Cheshire CW9 6ES
01606 41823
afielding@lionsalt.demon.co.uk
Traditionally mined Cheshire salt.

RPG Herbs
Smithy Lane, Hulme, Walfield, Congleton,
Cheshire CW12 2JG
01260 272418
www.rpgherbs.co.uk
Family run nursery specialising in culinary herbs
and unusual vegetable plants.

FLOUR

Bunbury Water Mill
Mill Lane, Bunbury, Cheshire CW6 9PP
01829 261422
www.bunbur-mill.org
Flour milling. Wholemeal and oatmeal.

Especially Delicious
66 North Crofts, Nantwich CW5 5SQ
01270 619 435
www.especiallydelicious.co.uk
Manufacturers of gluten and wheat free flour. A
unique combination of flours that makes delicious
food.

BOX SCHEMES

Northern Harvest
Kenyon Hall, Croft, Warrington, Cheshire WA3 7ED
01942 608 299
www.northernharvest.co.uk
Award-winning home delivery service and box
scheme, delivering to households and fine quality
restaurants throughout Cheshire and the North
West. Over 2,500 products available gathered in
from small scale growers and producers.

FARM SHOPS

Abbey Leys Farm
Peacock Lane, High Legh, Near Knutsford,
Cheshire WA16 6NS
01925 753465
www.abbeyleys.co.uk
Farm shop selling organic free range eggs,
potatoes, vegetables, fruit, cakes and preserves.

Alcumlow Hall Farm Shop
Alcumlow Hall, Astbury, Congleton,
Cheshire CW12 4TL
01260 299090
www.alcumlowhall.co.uk
Home to produced poultry, pork, lamb and beef,
free range eggs, home-cured bacon, pies, cheese,
vegetables and preserves.

Cheerbrook Quality Farm Foods Ltd
Cheerbrook Farm, Newcastle Road, Nantwich,
Cheshire CW5 7EL
01270 666431
shuff@cheerbrookfood.fsnet.co.uk
Quality farm shop with award-winning sausages
and butcher counter and new extended deli and
quality fruit and veg.

Cholmondeley Castle Farm Shop
Cholmondeley, Malpas, Cheshire SY14 8AQ
01829 720201
Farm/convenience shop. Suppliers of
Cholmondeley Estate produce. Longhorn beef,
venison and quality regional produce.

DJ Lowe and Partners
Shanty Farm, Byley, Middlewich,
Cheshire CW10 9NG
01606 832133
Growers of a wide range of vegetables and
potatoes, freshly picked every day for the farm
shop, complimented by other local produce.

DJ Witter and Co
Wheelock Hall Farm, Crewe Road, Sandbach,
Cheshire CW11 4RE
01270 764230
Farm shop, tearooms.

The Green Kitchen Garden
1 Hodge Lane, Gorstage Green, Weaverham,
Northwich CW8 2SF
01606 852 325
Market garden producing organic vegetables and
eggs. Everything is chemical, additive and pesticide
free. Also available are bedding plants, cut flowers
and fruit.

The Harvest Store
Hopley House, Wimboldsley, Middlewich,
Cheshire CW10 0LN
01270 526292
www.harveststore.co.uk
Farm shop selling quality local produce.

The Hollies Farm Shop
The Hollies, Forest Road, Little Budworth,
Near Tarporley CW6 9ES
01829 760414
Farm shop growing and selling high quality
vegetables, food and drink.

Holly Tree Farm Shop
Chester Road, Tabley, Knutsford,
Cheshire WA16 0EU
01565 651835
www.hollytreefarmshop.co.uk
Licensed butcher and licensed cutting room on site.
Licensed to cut other people's meat for resale by
them. Fresh meats, poultry, preserves, cakes, pies.

Horseshoe Farm Shop
Horseshoe Lane, Alderley Edge, Cheshire SK9 7QP
01625 590055
andyhorseshoefarm@tiscali.co.uk
Farm shop.

Little Heath Farm
Cow Lane, Dunham Massey,
Altrincham, Cheshire WA14 4SE
Farm shop.

Mollington Farms Limited
Grange Farm, Mollington CH1 6NP
01244 851 982
cjowade@aol.com
Farm shop and manufacturers of traditional English
cheeses.

Reaseheath College
Reaseheath, Nantwich CW5 6DF
01270 613 264
www.reaseheath.ac.uk
Farm shop.

Red Lion Farm
Main Road, Weston, Crewe CW2 5LD
Farm shop.

Rose Farm Shop
John Street, Utkinton, Tarporley, Cheshire CW6 0LP
01829 732978
www.rosefarmshop.co.uk
A small farm selling additive free beef. Also stocked
are farm sourced products: yoghurts, jams,
chutneys, pickles, fruit and veg and free range
eggs.

S and R Jones Farm Shop
New Farm, Lymm Road, Little Bollington,
Altrincham WA14 4SS
01565 830388
S-rjones@ic24.net
Homemade sponge cakes, fruit cakes, fruit pies,
bakewells, biscuits, shortbread and preserves.

JD Ford
Smithy Bank Farm, High Street, Norley, Frodsham,
Cheshire
01928 788398
Year round production and sale of a range of high
quality oriental vegetables and fruit grown from
oriental seed.

Teuthill Farm Shop
Teuthill Farm, Tarvin Road, Frodsham,
Cheshire WA6 6XH
01928 722622
www.teuthill.co.uk
Growers of potatoes (early new potatoes to main
crop), homemade cakes and pies. Potato peeling
and veg prep service for local hotels, restaurants
etc. Retailers of local produce.

FARMERS' MARKETS

Abbey Leys Farmers' Market
Abbey Leys Farm Shop, Peacock Lane, High Legh,
near Knutsford
01925 753 465
First Saturday monthly.

Altrincham Farmers' Market
Trafford Town Hall, Talbot Road, Stretford,
Altrincham, Cheshire
0161 9414261
First Friday in month.

Chester Regional Produce Market
Town Hall Square, Chester
01244 402 340
First Wednesday monthly.

Congleton Farmers' Market
Bridestones Centre (next to Safeway), Congleton
07739 529 225
Held on the first and third Tuesday of the month.

Crewe Farmers' Market
Municipal Square, Crewe
01270 537 805
Third Saturday monthly.

Ellesmere Port Farmers' Market
Adjoining Market Hall, Ellesmere Port
0151 356 6894
Fourth Saturday monthly.

The Harvest Store Farmers' Market
The Harvest Store, Hopley House, Wimboldsley,
Middlewich
01270 526 292
Second Sunday monthly.

Knutsford Farmers' Market
Silkmill Street, Knutsford, Cheshire
01625 504752
First Saturday monthly.

Matthew's Farmers' Market
Matthews Garden Centre, Alderley Park, Nether
Alderley, near Macclesfield (A34 Wilmslow to
Congleton Road)
01625 582 087
Second Sunday monthly.

Nantwich Farmers' Market
Nantwich Town Square, Cheshire
01270 537 805
Last Saturday monthly.

Northwich Farmers' Market
Apple Market Street, Weaver Square Shopping
Centre (outside traditional market), Northwich
01606 867 864
Second Sunday monthly.

Vale Royal Farmers' Market
Eddisbury Fruit Farm, Yeld Lane, Kelsall, Vale Royal,
Cheshire
01606 867 864
Third Saturday monthly.

Wrexham Farmers' Market
Queens Square, Wrexham, Cheshire
01978 292448
Third Friday monthly.

EATING PLACES

The Arkle
The Chester Grosvenor, Eastgate, Chester CH1 1LT
01244 324 024
www.chestergrosvenor.co.uk
A gourmet restaurant with a Michelin star. Local
produce used.

Delamere Station House Café
Station Road, Delamere, Northwich
01606 889825
Café.

Grosvenor Garden Centre
Wrexham Road, Belgrave, Chester,
Cheshire CH4 9EE
01244 625200
www.grosvenorgrdencentre.co.uk
Freshly made meals in the café.

Les's Fish Bar
51 Victoria Street, Crewe CW1 2JG
01270 257 581
Popular fish bar and café.

Les's Fish Bar
172 Widnes Road, Widnes WA8 6BL
0151 424 2444
Popular fish bar and café.

The Dysart Arms
Bowes Gate Road, Bunbury,
Near Tarporley CW9 6PH
01829 260183
www.dysartarms-bunbury.co.uk

Peppers Restaurant
Mill Street, Nantwich
01270 629 100
High quality restaurant which has a strong local
sourcing policy.